Published by:
The Junior League of Pasadena, Inc.

© The Junior League of Pasadena, Inc.
149 South Madison Avenue
Pasadena, California 91101

Edited and manufactured in the United
States of America by
Favorite Recipes® Press
an imprint of

FRP™

2451 Atrium Way
Nashville, Tennessee 37214

ISBN Number: 0-9632089-3-4
Library of Congress Number: 98-075003

First Printing, 1999
20,000

Cover photography by Cameron Carothers
Cover Graphic Design by Stacey Russakow
Cover Room Design by Diana Clark

Any inquiries about this book or orders for
additional copies should be directed to:
The Junior League of Pasadena, Inc.
626-796-0162

The Junior League of Pasadena, Inc., is an organization of women committed to promoting voluntarism, developing the potential of women, and improving the community through the effective action and leadership of trained volunteers. Its purpose is exclusively educational and charitable.

The focus of the Junior League of Pasadena is to nurture the children of our community by providing services that support the entire family. Within the past 72 years, the Junior League of Pasadena has contributed thousands upon thousands of volunteer hours and over $3 million to community projects including the arts, children's welfare, education, health, parenting, recreation, and women's issues.

Proceeds from the sale of *Dining by Design* will support the Junior League's indispensable work within the community for those in need.

Take a walk through these pages filled with mouthwatering recipes and photographs of strikingly beautiful decors. You'll see why Stylish Recipes and Savory Settings create such a wonderful combination! We started with a collection of our very favorite recipes, then sprinkled them with decorative interiors and landscapes to bridge the time we spend cooking at home with the lifestyles expressed by our homes.

In many ways, we all design our lives to reflect our true selves. Some of us live fast and furious while others choose to live at a slower pace. These choices are especially reflected in our cooking, with meals both simple and complex. Whichever lifestyle is you, *Dining by Design* gives plentiful ideas and options for celebrating with others and enhancing your time at home.

Hints and tips throughout the book help you to cook your midweek meal a little quicker or perhaps to prepare your formal dinner party with a little extra flair. Look for our suggestions on proper etiquette to help you through those tricky moments of entertaining.

For fun, browse through the family chapter. It features starter recipes for kids and dads (or moms) so everyone can help out in the kitchen. Learn the joy of cooking together . . . even if you have only a few ingredients and a moment to spare.

So meander with us through these pages and take a tour of the decorative settings we have selected to frame our favorite recipes and special cooking memories.
Enjoy!

"Master Chef"

Avery Dennison
BOS Design
The Original Farmers Market
"Meet Me at 3rd and Fairfax"
Cathy and Robert Woolway

"Bon Appetit"

Gail G. Ellis
Nancy and J. D. Hornberger
Amy and David Lamb
Charlene Conrad Liebau
Ann and Peter Murphy
Susie and Jim Rhodes
Linda and Fernando Roth

"Sous Chef"

Tali Arnold
June M. Banta
Kathleen Bertch
Jennifer and Franklin Bigelow
Mr. and Mrs. James Bolton
Diane Parker Coyer
Patty Duckett
Elizabeth Fitzpatrick
Mrs. John D. Gee
Glabman Furniture & Interior Design
Merrie and Thomas Gottschalk
Happy Trails Catering
Karen Kaiser
Laura and Brad Kelso
Helen Kerstein
Kathy Kimball
Rebecca Espinoza Kubacki
Jane Bucklin MacKinnon

Mrs. James W. McNabb
Milbank, Tweed, Hadley and McCloy
Nancy B. Munroe
Pallets of Plates
Penn Rice Consulting
Lori and Steve Phillipi
Dolores Romero
Katharine Carah Schlosberg
MaryAnn and Mike Smith
Mary and John Snider
Meshell and Michael Sohl
Pamela Hillings Tegtmeyer
The Knop Family
Jane and John Thompson
Sharon and Don Wright
Sally S. Wood
1998-99 Board of Directors

Special Menus

The Dining by Design Dinner Party

Three-Cheese and Mushroom Galette (page 24)
Butternut Squash Soup (page 80) or Pecan and Pear Salad
    with Bleu Cheese Dressing (page 89)
Prime Rib (page 164)
Green Beans and Peppers with Almonds (page 133)
Garlic Mashed Potatoes (page 141)
Lemon Torte (page 229)

Classic Italian Dinner

Italian Bread
Fresh Green Salad
Red Pepper Pasta (page 114)
Roasted Chicken with Fresh Herbs (page 179)
Peas with Pancetta (page 138)
Classic Italian Tiramisù (page 224)

Special Menus

Simple Meals

1. The Best Chinese Chicken Salad (page 107)
2. Hearty Sierra Chili (page 83)
3. Cashew Chicken Casserole (page 194)
4. Penne with Spicy Vodka Sauce (page 118)
Serve each one-dish entrée with a green salad
and/or fresh-baked bread from the local bakery.

Date Night with Your Sweetheart

Crab Salad in Endive (page 20)
Caribbean Swordfish with Thai Banana Salsa (page 208)
Steamed Broccoli
Crusty Bread
Zesty Lemon Mousse (page 231)
    or Almond Cognac Truffles (page 263)

Special Menus

Mother's Day Brunch

Cranberry Orange Scones (page 49) and/or Cappuccino Chip Muffins (page 50)
Newport Ham and Swiss Cheese Quiche (page 58)
   or Asparagus, Peppers and Gruyère Tart (page 57)
Planked Salmon with Spicy Red Pepper Relish (page 204)
Orzo Salad with Fresh Herbs (page 101)
Lemon Ricotta Dip for Strawberries (page 218)
Banana Brunch Cake (page 64)
Amber Tea (page 41)
Freshly Brewed Coffee

Holiday Open House

Appetizers
Basil and Tomato Torta (page 146)
Apricots with Gorgonzola (page 16)
Salmon Mousse (page 28)
Seasoned Brie Baked in Bread (page 30)
Spiced Almonds (page 35)
Desserts
Cranapple Crumble Pie (page 246)
Drunken Chocolate Pecan Cake (page 241)
Almond Citrus Biscotti (page 254)
Forgotten Cookies (page 257)

Special Menus

Neighborhood Block Party

Quick and Easy Salad with Spring Greens and Gorgonzola (page 92)
Fourth of July Baked Beans (page 133)
Marinated Flank Steak and/or Chicken with Classic Marinade (page 196)
Garlic Bread
Chocolate Sheet Cake (page 244)
Watermelon Slices

Best-Ever Slumber Party

For Dinner
Cheese Crisps (page 268)
Italian Cheese Toasts (page 268)
Carrot and Celery Sticks with Dip
Beef and Macaroni Delight (page 273)
    or Oven-Fried Drumsticks (page 278)
Ginger Water (page 287)
Banana Splits (page 290)
For Breakfast
Cinnamon Blueberry Muffins (page 269)
Breakfast Pizza (page 270)
Freshly Squeezed Orange Juice
For Party Favors
Cool Snappy Stretch (page 293)
Microwave Caramel Corn (page 288)
    (Wrap in cellophane and tie with a ribbon.)

At The Doorstep

Your entryway provides visitors with their first impression of your home. In the same way, appetizers provide your guests with their first impression of a meal or party. Follow the recipes in this chapter, and when the doorbell rings, these tantalizing tastes will welcome guests into your home.

**Designer
Caroline
Baker**

**Photographer
Cameron
Carothers**

Pasadena Showcase
House of Design

Chicken Wings Pacifica

Easy dish to make ahead.

1	cup soy sauce	3/4	cup water
1	cup packed brown sugar	3	pounds chicken wings or
1/2	cup butter or margarine		drummettes
1	teaspoon dry mustard		

Combine the soy sauce, brown sugar, butter, mustard and water in a saucepan. Cook over low heat until the butter is melted and the brown sugar is dissolved. Let cool.

Arrange the chicken in a shallow baking dish. Pour the soy sauce mixture over the chicken. Marinate, covered, in the refrigerator for 2 to 10 hours, turning occasionally.

Preheat the oven to 350 degrees. Bake the chicken, uncovered, for 1 hour or until cooked through, turning once and basting occasionally. Remove to a plate lined with paper towels; drain.

May be served hot or cold.

Yield: 6 servings

Prosciutto Pinwheels

A perfect start for any dinner party.

1¼	cups shredded Gruyère cheese	1	sheet frozen puff pastry, thawed
5	teaspoons chopped fresh	1	large egg, lightly beaten
	Sage leaves	1½	ounces thinly sliced prosciutto

Combine the Gruyère cheese and sage in a bowl. Arrange the pastry sheet, short side facing you, on a lightly floured surface; cut into halves crosswise. Place one half-sheet with long side facing you; brush the edge of the far side with the egg.

Layer with half the prosciutto and Gruyère cheese mixture, avoiding the egg-moistened edge. Roll up jelly-roll fashion, shaping into a log. Wrap in waxed paper. Repeat the process with the remaining pastry, prosciutto and cheese mixture. Chill, seam side down, in the refrigerator for 3 hours to 3 days or until firm.

Preheat the oven to 400 degrees. Grease 2 large baking sheets. Cut the logs crosswise into ½-inch slices. Arrange, cut side down, 1 inch apart on the baking sheets.

Bake, in batches, on the middle oven rack for 14 to 16 minutes or until golden. Remove to a wire rack to cool slightly. Serve warm.

Yield: 40 pinwheels

Apricots with Gorgonzola

Looks beautiful arranged on a serving tray.

32	pecan or walnut halves	32	dried apricot halves
5	ounces Gorgonzola cheese	3	tablespoons minced fresh mint
1½	teaspoons pepper, or to taste		

Place the pecans in a small skillet over medium heat. Cook for 4 minutes or until toasted, shaking the skillet frequently to prevent scorching. Let cool.

Combine the cheese and pepper in a food processor bowl. Process until combined. Spoon into the apricots. Press 1 pecan into each.

Place the mint in a shallow bowl. Dip the apricots, cheese side down, into the mint, pressing gently. Arrange on a serving platter, cheese side up.

Hint: May be made ahead and stored, covered, in the refrigerator for up to 4 hours.

Yield: 12 servings

Quick Cheese Toasts

1	cup mayonnaise	1	to 2 teaspoons freshly ground
1	small onion, minced		pepper
2	tablespoons grated Parmesan cheese	1	baguette, thinly sliced
		¼	cup minced fresh parsley

Preheat the oven to 375 degrees.

Whisk the mayonnaise, onion, cheese and pepper in a small bowl. Spread on baguette slices. Arrange on a baking sheet.

Bake for 7 to 8 minutes or until golden. Top with the parsley.

Yield: 32 appetizers

Eggplant Spread on Parmesan Toasts

A healthful appetizer that's sure to please all appetites.

Spread
1/4 cup pine nuts
2 cloves garlic
6 tablespoons olive oil
1 eggplant (about 1 1/4 pounds), cut into 1/2-inch cubes
1 onion, chopped
 Salt to taste
1/2 teaspoon salt
3 tomatoes (about 3/4 pound), cut into 1/2-inch cubes
1/2 cup packed fresh basil leaves, chopped

1/3 cup packed fresh parsley leaves, chopped
3 tablespoons lemon juice
1/2 teaspoon sugar
 Freshly ground pepper

Toasts
1/4 cup olive oil
1 baguette (about 15 inches long), cut diagonally into 1/4-inch slices
1/3 cup grated Parmesan cheese

For the spread, place the pine nuts on a baking sheet. Toast at 350 degrees for 5 to 10 minutes or until lightly browned.

Mince 1 garlic clove. Warm 3 tablespoons of the oil in a large heavy skillet over medium-high heat for 1 minute. Add the eggplant, onion, minced garlic and salt to taste. Sauté until the eggplant begins to brown. Reduce the heat to medium. Cook, covered, for 10 minutes or until the eggplant is tender, stirring occasionally. Transfer to a bowl; let cool.

Chop and mash the remaining garlic clove and 1/2 teaspoon salt into a paste. Stir into the eggplant mixture. Add the tomatoes, basil, parsley, lemon juice, sugar, remaining 3 tablespoons oil, and salt and pepper to taste. Stir the pine nuts into the eggplant mixture just before serving.

Hint: May be made ahead and stored, covered, in the refrigerator for up to 2 days. Bring to room temperature before using.

For the toasts, preheat the oven to 325 degrees. Brush the oil over both sides of each bread slice. Arrange the slices in a single layer on a baking sheet. Place on the middle oven rack. Toast for 15 minutes. Turn the slices; sprinkle with the cheese. Toast for 15 minutes or until golden. Remove to a wire rack; let cool. Spread the eggplant mixture over the toasts just before serving.

Hint: May be made ahead and stored in a sealable plastic bag for up to 2 days.

Yield: 45 appetizers

Garlic Prawns

Be ready for the garlic.

1/4	cup red wine vinegar
1/4	cup tarragon vinegar
1/2	cup olive oil
1/4	cup finely chopped fresh parsley
1/4	cup finely chopped shallots
4	teaspoons Dijon mustard
8	small cloves garlic, minced
1	to 2 teaspoons crushed red pepper flakes
1	to 2 pounds frozen cooked prawns or large shrimp, thawed

Whisk the wine vinegar, tarragon vinegar, oil, parsley, shallots, mustard, garlic and pepper in a small bowl.

Place the prawns in a shallow baking dish. Pour in the vinegar mixture. Marinate, covered, in the refrigerator for 6 to 10 hours. May be served with sliced baguette toasts.

Yield: 8 servings

Cheese and Food Complements

Gruyère	fresh fruit
Mozzarella	Italian foods
Muenster	crackers, bread
Parmesan	Italian foods
Provolone	Italian foods
Ricotta	Italian foods
Swiss	fresh fruit, French bread
Bleu	fresh fruit, bland crackers
Brie	fresh fruit
Camembert	apples
Cheddar	fresh fruit, crackers
Edam	fresh fruit
Feta	Greek salad
Gorgonzola	fresh fruit, Italian bread
Gouda	fresh fruit, crackers

Designer
Michaela
Scherrer

Photographer
Michael E.
Garland

Pasadena Showcase
House of Design

Crab Salad in Endive

6 ounces crab meat, well drained
1/2 cup frozen corn kernels, thawed
1/4 cup finely chopped red onion
1/4 cup mayonnaise
4 teaspoons mixed chopped fresh herbs (such as chervil, tarragon, parsley)
1 tablespoon thawed frozen orange juice concentrate
1 tablespoon fresh lemon juice
1 teaspoon grated lemon peel
1/2 teaspoon ground cumin
1/4 teaspoon cayenne
Salt and pepper to taste
2 heads Belgian endive, separated into spears
1 tablespoon finely chopped fresh parsley
Paprika

Combine the crab meat, corn, red onion, mayonnaise, fresh herbs, orange juice concentrate, lemon juice, lemon peel, cumin and cayenne in a medium bowl. Season with the salt and pepper.

Chill, covered, in the refrigerator for up to 1 day.

Drain the salad. Place 1 rounded tablespoonful in the base end of each endive spear. Sprinkle the parsley and paprika over each serving. Arrange on a platter.

Yield: 10 servings

Hot Crab and Artichoke Dip

A zesty variation of the traditional artichoke dip.

1½ teaspoons olive oil
½ medium red bell pepper, chopped
1 (14-ounce) can artichoke hearts, drained, chopped
¾ cup mayonnaise
⅓ cup grated Parmesan cheese
¼ cup thinly sliced green onions
1 tablespoon Worcestershire sauce

1 tablespoon finely chopped pickled jalapeño chiles (optional)
1½ teaspoons lemon juice
½ teaspoon celery salt
8 ounces crab meat, drained
Salt and pepper to taste
Assorted crackers
Baguette slices, warmed

Preheat the oven to 375 degrees.

Warm the oil in a medium nonstick skillet over medium-high heat. Add the bell pepper. Sauté for 3 minutes or until light brown. Remove to a large bowl.

Stir in the artichoke hearts, mayonnaise, Parmesan cheese, green onions, Worcestershire sauce, jalapeño, lemon juice and celery salt. Mix in the crab. Season with the salt and pepper.

Remove the mixture to an 8-inch-diameter quiche or pie pan with a 1½-inch-high side, spreading evenly.

Bake for 30 minutes or until the top is light golden brown and bubbly. Serve warm with the crackers and warmed baguette slices.

Yield: 8 servings

Amazing Bleu Cheese Appetizer

Even those who are not lovers of bleu cheese will enjoy this dish.

12	ounces bleu cheese
4	cloves garlic, crushed
1/2	cup olive oil
4	tablespoons red wine vinegar
2	tablespoons lemon juice
1	cup chopped red onion
1	cup minced fresh cilantro

Crumble the bleu cheese evenly over the bottom of a tart dish. Whisk the garlic and olive oil in a measuring cup. Drizzle over the cheese.

Combine the vinegar, lemon juice, onion and cilantro in a bowl. Spread over the cheese mixture.Chill, covered, in the refrigerator for 2 hours.

May be served with tart apple slices and wheat biscuit crackers.

Yield: 10 servings

Baked Mozzarella Toasts

3 tablespoons olive oil
12 to 16 slices ($1/4$ inch thick)
   mozzarella cheese
   Freshly ground white pepper
2 tablespoons butter
1 baguette, bias cut into 12 to
   16 ($1/4$-inch) slices

$1/2$ cup pesto sauce
2 to 3 red bell peppers, roasted,
   sliced (optional)
2 to 3 yellow bell peppers,
   roasted, sliced (optional)

Brush the oil over the cheese slices. Sprinkle with the pepper. Marinate, covered, in the refrigerator for 1 to 10 hours.

Preheat the oven to 375 degrees. Spread the butter over the baguette slices. Arrange on a baking sheet. Toast in the oven until golden. Top each with a mozzarella slice. Bake for 5 minutes or just until the cheese begins to melt. Remove to a serving platter.

Drizzle the pesto sauce over each toast, and top with strips of bell pepper.

Hint: May use bell peppers in other colors; green and red are especially nice for the holidays. May substitute salad greens tossed with balsamic vinaigrette for the peppers.

Yield: 8 servings

Three-Cheese and Mushroom Galette

1	tablespoon butter
6	mushrooms, sliced
1	small onion, thinly sliced
3	cloves garlic, sliced
2	teaspoons minced fresh oregano
	Salt and pepper to taste
1	(15-ounce) package refrigerated pie crusts
1/2	cup ricotta cheese
1	cup shredded Monterey Jack cheese
1/2	cup shredded smoked mozzarella cheese
1	egg, beaten
2	tablespoons water
1	green onion, chopped

Melt the butter in a skillet over medium heat. Add the mushrooms, onion and garlic. Sauté for 2 to 3 minutes or until softened. Stir in the oregano. Season with the salt and pepper.

Stack the pie crusts on a lightly floured work surface. Roll to 16-inch round. Slide onto a baking sheet.

Spread the ricotta cheese over the pastry, leaving a 3-inch border. Distribute the mushroom mixture evenly over the ricotta. Sprinkle the Monterey Jack and mozzarella cheeses over the mushrooms. Fold pastry rim to partially cover the filling, forming soft pleats where the dough overlaps.

Preheat the oven to 400 degrees. Whisk the egg and water in a small bowl. Brush over the pastry. Bake for 25 minutes. Sprinkle the green onion over the cheese. Bake for 10 minutes or until golden brown.

May be served hot or at room temperature.

Yield: 6 servings

Traditional Salsa

2¼ pounds plum tomatoes, seeded, finely chopped
1 large onion, finely chopped
¾ cup chopped fresh cilantro

5 cloves garlic, minced
3 jalapeño chiles, seeded, minced
3 tablespoons lime juice
Salt and pepper to taste

Combine the tomatoes, onion, cilantro, garlic, jalapeños and lime juice in a bowl. Season with salt and pepper.

Chill, covered, for 1 to 4 hours before serving.

Yield: about 5 cups

Tangy Tofu Dip

Everyone will love this. Try it.

½ teaspoon Tabasco sauce
¼ cup coarsely chopped yellow onion
5 green onions, coarsely chopped
2 or 3 cloves garlic, peeled
¼ cup extra-virgin olive oil
¼ cup lemon juice

½ teaspoon hot curry powder
½ teaspoon cumin
½ teaspoon salt
3 grinds of pepper
1½ tablespoons black soy sauce
1½ tablespoons balsamic vinegar
1 (14-ounce) package firm tofu, rinsed, drained

Combine the Tabasco sauce, onion, green onions, garlic, olive oil, lemon juice, curry powder, cumin, salt, pepper, soy sauce and balsamic vinegar in a food processor bowl. Process until puréed and well blended. Pat the tofu dry with paper towels. Add the tofu to the puréed mixture. Process until smooth.

Serve with pieces of pita pocket bread for dipping or use instead of mayonnaise on sandwiches and hamburgers.

Yield: about 2 cups

Crab-Filled French Bread

1   loaf French bread, cut lengthwise into halves
8   ounces sharp Cheddar cheese, shredded
2   or 3 green onions
1   tablespoon butter, softened
2   tablespoons mayonnaise
   Lemon juice to taste
6   ounces crab meat
3   tablespoons chopped fresh cilantro

Preheat the oven to 350 degrees.

Remove a small portion of the bread center to create a shallow indentation in each half.

Combine the Cheddar cheese, green onions and butter in a food processor bowl or blender jar. Process until blended. Spread the mixture on the bread halves.

Combine the mayonnaise, lemon juice and crab meat in a bowl. Spread over the cheese mixture.

Bake for 20 minutes or until bubbly. Sprinkle the cilantro over the crab meat mixture. Cut into serving-size pieces. Serve immediately.

Yield: 6 servings

Salmon Mousse

1	(10¾-ounce) can condensed tomato soup	1	cup minced celery
8	ounces cream cheese	¼	to ½ cup minced onion
1	cup mayonnaise	1	to 2 tablespoons minced fresh parsley
2	envelopes unflavored gelatin	1	tablespoon fresh dill
¼	cup cold water		Pepper to taste
2	(6½-ounce) cans boneless, skinless pink salmon, flaked		Vegetable oil

Combine the soup and cream cheese in a large saucepan. Cook over low heat until the cheese is melted. Remove from the heat. Whisk in the mayonnaise.

Soften the gelatin in the water in a small bowl. Stir into the tomato-cheese mixture. Stir in the salmon, celery, onion, parsley, dill and pepper.

Oil a mold or medium bundt pan. Pour the mixture into the mold. Cover with plastic wrap and foil. Chill in the refrigerator for 8 to 36 hours. Dip the mold into warm water to loosen the mousse; turn onto a serving plate.

May be garnished with parsley and served with bread or crackers.

Yield: 10 servings

Italian Torte

This makes a hearty appetizer, which looks great on a buffet table garnished with fresh basil.

1	package (16 to 20) sun-dried tomatoes	1/2	cup pesto
12	slices provolone cheese	16	ounces cream cheese, softened
		1	to 2 cloves garlic, minced

Place the tomatoes in a medium-size bowl and pour in enough boiling water to cover. Let stand for 8 to 10 minutes or until softened. Drain well. Chop finely.

Cut a piece of cheesecloth large enough to cover the bottom and sides as well as extend over the top of a loaf pan. Dampen with water and arrange in the pan.

Line the pan with 4 slices of the provolone cheese, covering the entire bottom and sides of the pan by overlapping the slices. Spread half the pesto over the provolone.

Combine the cream cheese and garlic in a bowl. Layer 1/2 of the cream cheese mixture, 1/2 of the tomatoes and 1/2 of the provolone in the prepared pan. Spread with the remaining 1/4 cup pesto. Layer the remaining cream cheese mixture, tomatoes and provolone cheese over the top.

Pull the cheesecloth tightly across the top; press down to remove excess oil and to mold the torte to the pan. Chill in the refrigerator for at least 4 hours. Bring to room temperature before serving. Turn out on serving platter and remove cheesecloth. Serve with crackers or sliced bread.

Hint: May be stored in the refrigerator for up to 3 days. May use sun-dried tomatoes packed in oil, drained and rinsed well instead of the packaged sun-dried tomatoes.

Yield: 10 servings

Seasoned Brie Baked in Bread

Works well on the buffet table.

10	to 12 ounces Brie cheese, softened
8	ounces cream cheese, softened
1	tablespoon olive oil
1/2	medium onion, chopped
2	cloves garlic, chopped
3/4	cup sour cream
2	teaspoons Worcestershire sauce
2	tablespoons brown sugar
2	teaspoons lemon juice
1	round loaf bread
	Crudités (red and green bell pepper, broccoli, green beans, and so forth)

Combine the Brie cheese and cream cheese in a large bowl.

Warm the oil in a skillet over medium-high heat. Add the onion and garlic. Sauté until softened. Stir into the cheese mixture. Add the sour cream, Worcestershire sauce, brown sugar and lemon juice; mix well.

Slice the top off the bread. Hollow out the loaf, leaving a sturdy shell and reserving the bread chunks for dipping. Spoon the cheese mixture into the bread shell. Replace the top. Wrap in heavy-duty foil.

Preheat the oven to 400 degrees. Bake for 1 hour. Serve with the crudités and bread chunks.

Yield: 10 servings

Baked Brie Topped with Caramelized Onions

Serve this rich appetizer with assorted crudités and mulled wine.
Be sure to use an uncut wheel of cheese.

1	tablespoon butter	1/2	teaspoon sugar
4	cups sliced onions (about 4 large)		Salt and pepper to taste
1/2	tablespoon minced fresh thyme	1	(4-inch-diameter, 16- to 18-ounce) French Brie cheese, packed in wooden box
2	cloves garlic, chopped		
4	tablespoons dry white wine	1	baguette, sliced

Melt the butter in a large heavy skillet over medium-high heat. Add the onions. Sauté for 6 minutes or until tender. Add the thyme. Reduce the heat to medium. Cook for 25 minutes or until golden brown, stirring often.

Stir in the garlic. Sauté for 2 minutes. Stir in 2 tablespoons of the wine. Cook for 2 minutes or until almost all the liquid evaporates, stirring constantly. Sprinkle the sugar over the onions. Sauté for 10 minutes or until soft and brown. Stir in the remaining 2 tablespoons wine. Cook for 2 minutes or just until the liquid evaporates, stirring constantly. Season with salt and pepper. Let cool.

Preheat the oven to 350 degrees. Unwrap the Brie, reserving the bottom of the box. Cut off the top rind. Return to the box rind side down. Place on a baking sheet. Top with the onion mixture.

Bake for 30 minutes or just until the cheese melts. Remove the box to a platter. Serve with the baguette slices.

Hint: The onions may be made ahead and stored, covered, in the refrigerator for up to 2 days.

Yield: 6 servings

Red Pepper Pesto with Crostini

The pesto is a unique combination of ingredients that would also be nice with pasta.

1	(7-ounce) jar roasted red peppers, drained		Pinch of ground cinnamon
1/2	cup fresh cilantro leaves	1/2	cup (about 2 1/2 ounces) whole toasted almonds
6	tablespoons olive oil		Salt and pepper to taste
3	tablespoons balsamic vinegar	1	French or sourdough baguette, cut into 1/4- to 1/3-inch slices, toasted
1	small clove garlic, chopped		
1/2	teaspoon dry mustard		
1/2	teaspoon ground coriander		

Combine the peppers, cilantro, oil, vinegar, garlic, mustard, coriander and cinnamon in a food processor bowl. Process until almost smooth. Add the almonds. Process until the almonds are finely chopped but not ground. Season with salt and pepper. Serve with the crostini.

Yield: 10 servings

Spinach Artichoke Dip

2	tablespoons butter	1	(14-ounce) can artichoke hearts, drained, chopped
1/2	onion, finely chopped		
3	cloves garlic, or to taste	2/3	cup grated Romano cheese
2	(10-ounce) packages frozen chopped spinach	8	ounces shredded Monterey Jack cheese
4	ounces cream cheese, softened		Tortilla chips
1	cup sour cream		

Preheat the oven to 350 degrees. Melt the butter in a large skillet over medium-high heat. Add the onion and garlic. Sauté until softened. Cook the spinach according to package directions; drain. Squeeze dry with paper towels.

Stir the spinach, cream cheese, sour cream and artichokes into the onion mixture. Remove from the heat. Stir in the Romano cheese and half the Monterey Jack cheese. Spoon into a shallow baking dish; top with the remaining Monterey Jack cheese. Bake for 15 to 20 minutes or until the cheese is melted. Serve with tortilla chips.

Yield: 6 servings

Olive Cheese Ball

8	ounces cream cheese, softened	2/3	cup chopped black olives
8	ounces Danish bleu cheese, crumbled	1	tablespoon minced chives
1/4	cup butter or margarine, softened	1/3	cup chopped walnuts

Combine the cream cheese, bleu cheese, butter, olives and chives in a bowl. Form into a ball. Roll the ball in the walnuts.

Chill, covered, in the refrigerator. Serve with assorted crackers.

Yield: 8 servings

Swiss Cheese Spread

This will be a surprise hit for any occasion. Must be made one day ahead.

3/4	pound Swiss cheese, shredded	1/4	cup mayonnaise
2	hard-cooked eggs, chopped		Chopped parsley
1	large onion slice, minced		

Combine the Swiss cheese, eggs, onion and mayonnaise in a bowl.

Chill, covered, in the refrigerator for at least 10 hours. Mound onto a serving plate. Top with the parsley. Serve with assorted crackers.

Yield: 10 servings

Spiced Almonds

Pack these nuts in a decorative tin and tie it with a bow for a perfect hostess gift.
Prepare before an open house and set the mood with the spicy aroma.

1/2	teaspoon ground cumin		1/4	teaspoon ground cinnamon
1/2	teaspoon chili powder		2	tablespoons olive oil
1/2	teaspoon curry powder		2	cups shelled whole almonds or pecans
1/2	teaspoon garlic salt			
1/4	teaspoon cayenne		1	tablespoon coarse (kosher) salt (optional)
1/4	teaspoon powdered ginger			

Preheat the oven to 325 degrees.

Combine the cumin, chili powder, curry powder, garlic salt, cayenne, ginger and cinnamon in a small bowl. Warm the oil in a nonstick skillet over low heat. Add the spice mixture; stir well. Cook for 3 to 4 minutes to blend flavors.

Combine the almonds and spice mixture in a medium bowl; mix well. Spread in a single layer on a baking sheet.

Bake for 15 minutes, shaking the baking sheet once or twice. Do not overbake; almonds burn easily. Remove from the oven. Stir the almonds to mix with any spices and oil on the baking sheet. Sprinkle the salt and additional garlic salt over the almonds. Let cool for 2 hours. Store in airtight containers.

Yield: 2 cups

- *Any celebration deserves a toast, and the proper time to deliver it is after dessert has been served and Champagne glasses filled.*
- *A toast should be short and to the point, humorous if possible, and delivered by someone who is sober.*
- *The host should stand (if it is a large group), smile, and make the remarks. The honoree does not drink to herself. She may reciprocate with her own toast of thanks and may then drink.*
- *If you do not drink, raise your water glass in tribute.*

**Designer
Lauren Elia**

**Photographer
Cameron
Carothers**

Cosmopolitan Cocktail

3	scoops ice cubes
1/4	cup vodka
3	teaspoons cranberry juice
	Juice of 1/2 lime
2	thin strips lime peel

Place the ice, vodka, cranberry juice and lime juice in a cocktail shaker. Shake to mix well.

Serve, garnished with the lime peel, in martini glasses.

Yield: 2 servings

Sconces & Scones

Bedrooms are designed for you to start each day with a smile and to send you on your way. Treat yourself once in a while to a leisurely breakfast in bed, which will surely add a relaxing tone to your day.

Designer
Diana Clark

Photographer
Cameron
Carothers

43

Whole cloves are ideal for ham and pork, pot roasts, stews, and pickled fruits. For an aromatic holiday decoration, pierce an orange with cloves, completely covering the fruit.

Ground cloves can be used in spice cake and cookies, chocolate desserts, beets, sweet potatoes, onions, and winter squash.

Pumpkin Chocolate Chip Bread

	Nonstick cooking spray
	Flour for dusting
3	cups flour
3	cups sugar
2	teaspoons baking soda
1/2	teaspoon baking powder
1	teaspoon salt
1	teaspoon cloves
1	teaspoon allspice
1	teaspoon cinnamon
1	cup vegetable oil
4	eggs
2/3	cup water
2	cups canned pumpkin
2	cups chocolate chips

Preheat the oven to 325 degrees. Coat two 5x9-inch loaf pans with the cooking spray. Dust with the flour.

Combine the 3 cups flour, sugar, baking soda, baking powder, salt, cloves, allspice and cinnamon in a large bowl. Whisk the oil, eggs and water in a medium bowl. Add to the flour mixture; mix well. Add the pumpkin and chocolate chips; mix just until combined.

Divide the batter between the pans. Bake for 1¼ hours or until a wooden pick inserted in the center comes out clean. Remove from the pans; cool on a wire rack.

Yield: 2 loaves

British Country Scones

1/2	cup dried currants	5	tablespoons butter or margarine
2	cups flour	8	ounces sour cream
3	tablespoons plus 1 teaspoon sugar	1	egg yolk
2	teaspoons baking powder		Flour for kneading
3/4	teaspoon salt	1	egg white, slightly beaten
1/2	teaspoon baking soda	1/8	teaspoon cinnamon

Preheat the oven to 400 degrees. Place the currants in a small bowl, and pour in enough hot water to cover. Let stand until softened; drain.

Combine the 2 cups flour, 3 tablespoons of the sugar, baking powder, salt and baking soda in a large bowl. Cut in the butter with a pastry blender until the mixture resembles coarse crumbs. Mix in the currants.

Combine the sour cream and egg yolk in a small bowl. Add to the flour mixture, stirring until the dough clings together.

Turn out onto a lightly floured work surface. Knead for 10 to 12 strokes. Pat into a 1/2-inch-thick circle, and cut into 5 small circles. Slice each circle into quarters. Do not separate the quarters.

Place on an ungreased baking sheet. Brush the egg white over the top of each. Combine the cinnamon and remaining 1 teaspoon sugar in a small bowl. Sprinkle over each scone.

Bake for 15 to 18 minutes or until the scones are golden.

Yield: 20 scones

Cranberry Orange Scones

Nonstick cooking spray
1 cup all-purpose flour
1 cup sifted cake flour
2/3 cup sugar plus 2 teaspoons sugar
2 teaspoons baking powder
1/2 teaspoon baking soda
1/4 teaspoon salt
3 tablespoons margarine, chilled, cut into small pieces
3/4 cup frozen cranberries, thawed, halved
2 teaspoons grated orange peel
3/4 cup plain nonfat yogurt
Flour for kneading

Preheat the oven to 450 degrees. Coat a baking sheet with the cooking spray.

Combine the all-purpose flour, cake flour, 2/3 cup sugar, baking powder, baking soda and salt in a bowl. Cut in the margarine with a pastry blender or 2 knives until the mixture resembles coarse crumbs. Mix in the cranberries and orange peel. Add the yogurt, stirring just until the dry ingredients are moistened. The dough will be sticky.

Turn out onto a lightly floured work surface. Knead 4 or 5 strokes, using floured hands. Remove to the baking sheet. Pat into an 8-inch circle, and cut into 12 wedges. Do not separate the wedges. Sprinkle the remaining 2 teaspoons sugar over the top of the dough.

Bake for 12 minutes or until golden. Serve warm.

Yield: 12 scones

Remodel Your Scone

Like other types of breads, scones can be designed to suit your taste. Plain scones are traditionally served with preserves, lemon curd, and clotted cream. For additional variations, however, use the British Country Scones recipe on page 47, omitting the currants, and try adding any of the following to the batter before baking: chocolate, butterscotch, or peanut butter morsels; dried fruits and toasted nuts; a crushed candy bar; Cheddar cheese and green chiles; cooked ham and Swiss cheese; macadamia nuts and pineapple; fruit purée; or cinnamon and raisins.

Designer
Lois Mahar

Photographer
Alexander
Vertikoff

Cappuccino Chip Muffins

Nonstick cooking spray
1$^1/_2$ cups flour
$^3/_4$ tablespoon baking powder
$^1/_4$ teaspoon salt
1 large egg
$^1/_4$ cup sugar
$^3/_4$ cup milk

3 teaspoons instant espresso coffee dissolved in 1 teaspoon water
6 tablespoons melted unsalted butter
$^3/_4$ teaspoon vanilla extract
$^1/_2$ cup chocolate chips

Preheat the oven to 375 degrees. Coat muffin cups with the cooking spray.

Sift the flour, baking powder and salt into a large bowl. Whisk the egg, sugar, milk, espresso mixture, butter and vanilla in a medium bowl. Add to the flour mixture, mixing just until combined. Fold in the chocolate chips.

Fill the muffin cups $^2/_3$ full. Bake for 30 minutes or until a wooden pick inserted into the center of a muffin comes out clean.

Yield: 12 muffins

Cranberry Bran Muffins

Nonstick cooking spray
1 cup boiling water
3 cups bran flakes
2 1/2 cups flour
1 1/2 cups sugar
2 teaspoons baking soda

1/4 teaspoon salt
2 cups buttermilk
1/2 cup vegetable oil
2 large eggs
1 cup dried cranberries

Preheat the oven to 350 degrees. Coat muffin cups with the cooking spray. Combine the boiling water and 1 cup of the bran flakes. Let stand until cool.

Combine the remaining 2 cups bran flakes, flour, sugar, baking soda and salt in a large bowl. Whisk the buttermilk, oil and eggs in a small bowl. Add to the flour mixture, mixing just until combined. Stir in the moistened bran flakes and the cranberries.

Fill the muffin cups 2/3 full. Bake for 20 minutes or until a wooden pick inserted into the center of a muffin comes out clean.

Hint: If you do not have any buttermilk available, use 2 tablespoons vinegar plus enough milk to equal 2 cups. Let stand 10 minutes.

Yield: 12 muffins

Macadamia Nut Muffins

1 cup plus 2 tablespoons bread flour
1 1/4 teaspoons baking powder
1/2 teaspoon salt
1/2 cup unsalted butter, softened
1 cup packed brown sugar
3 large eggs

3/4 teaspoon almond extract
1/2 teaspoon vanilla extract
1/4 cup whipping cream
3/4 cup (about 3 3/4 ounces) coarsely chopped macadamia nuts
1/3 cup whole macadamia nuts

Preheat the oven to 350 degrees. Line 10 muffin cups with paper liners. Sift the flour, baking powder and salt into a medium bowl.

Beat the butter and brown sugar in a large mixer bowl to blend. Add the eggs; mix well. Beat in the almond and vanilla extracts. Add the flour mixture; beat until combined. Add the whipping cream; beat just until smooth. Fold in the chopped nuts.

Divide the batter among the muffin cups. Top with the whole nuts. Bake for 25 minutes or until a wooden pick inserted into the center of a muffin comes out clean. Serve warm or at room temperature.

Yield: 10 muffins

Bed and Breakfast Granola

This fantastic granola is perfect over yogurt and ice cream, as cereal or even as a snack.

3	cups rolled oats	1/2	cup packed brown sugar
3/4	cup coarsely chopped pecans	1/4	cup water
3/4	cup coarsely chopped almonds	3	tablespoons vegetable oil
1/2	cup shredded coconut	1	cup golden raisins
1/2	cup molasses	1	cup dried cranberries

Preheat the oven to 325 degrees.

Combine the oats, pecans, almonds and coconut in a 12x17-inch nonstick jelly roll pan. Combine the molasses, brown sugar, water and oil in a saucepan. Bring to a boil. Pour over the oat mixture; mix well. Bake for 20 minutes, stirring every 5 minutes.

Stir in the raisins and cranberries. Bake for 15 minutes, stirring every 5 minutes. Let cool. Store in an airtight container.

Yield: 7 cups

Following Pages

Designer
Judy Campbell

Photographer
Phillip Nilsson

Artichoke and Smoked Ham Strata

Butter
2 cups milk
$1/4$ cup olive oil
8 cups 1-inch cubes sourdough bread, crusts trimmed
$1^1/2$ cups whipping cream
5 large eggs
1 tablespoon chopped garlic
$1^1/2$ teaspoons salt
$3/4$ teaspoon white pepper
$1/2$ teaspoon ground nutmeg
12 ounces soft fresh goat cheese, crumbled

2 tablespoons chopped fresh sage
1 tablespoon chopped fresh thyme
$1^1/2$ teaspoons herbes de Provence
12 ounces smoked ham, chopped
3 ($6^1/2$-ounce) jars marinated artichoke hearts, drained, halved lengthwise
1 cup packed shredded fontina cheese
$1^1/2$ cups packed grated Parmesan cheese

Preheat the oven to 350 degrees. Butter a 9x13-inch baking dish.

Whisk the milk and oil in a large bowl. Stir in the bread. Let stand for 10 minutes or until the liquid is absorbed.

Whisk the cream, eggs, garlic, salt, pepper and nutmeg in another large bowl to blend. Stir in the goat cheese. Combine the sage, thyme and herbes de Provence in a small bowl.

Arrange half the bread mixture in the baking dish. Layer with half the ham, artichokes, herbs and fontina and Parmesan cheeses. Pour half the cream mixture over the top. Repeat the layers, starting with the bread and ending with the cream mixture.

Bake, uncovered, for 1 hour or until firm in the center and brown around the edges.

Hint: Herbes de Provence can be found in most supermarkets; a combination of dried basil, savory and fennel seeds may be substituted for the herbes de Provence. May be made 1 day ahead and stored, covered, in the refrigerator. Bake before serving.

Yield: 8 servings

**Designer
Edward
Turrentine**

French Toast with Maple Cream

French Toast
3   large eggs
1/4   cup milk
1/8   teaspoon salt
1/8   teaspoon pepper
1/8   teaspoon cinnamon
1/8   teaspoon nutmeg
     Nonstick cooking spray
1   loaf challa raisin bread, sliced

Maple Cream
1/2   cup maple syrup
1/2   cup water
2   egg whites
1   teaspoon lemon juice
1/2   cup whipping cream, whipped
     to stiff peaks
1/2   cup chopped pecans, toasted

For the French toast, whisk the eggs, milk, salt, pepper, cinnamon and nutmeg in a medium bowl.

Coat a griddle with the cooking spray; heat. Dip the bread slices in the egg mixture, turning to coat each side. Arrange on the griddle. Cook until the bottom of each slice is light golden brown. Turn. Brown the other side. Remove to a platter, and cover with foil. Keep warm in the oven.

For the cream, combine the syrup and water in a small heavy-bottomed saucepan. Bring to a boil over high heat. Reduce the heat to medium. Boil for 5 to 10 minutes or until the mixture reaches the soft-ball (or spin-a-thread) stage (236 degrees on a candy thermometer).

Beat the egg whites with the lemon juice until the whites form stiff peaks but are still moist. Beat the syrup slowly into the egg whites until thoroughly mixed. Fold in the whipped cream.

Arrange the French toast on individual plates. Serve with the maple cream and garnish with the pecans.

Hint: The pecans may be toasted in a 350-degree oven for 5 minutes. The maple cream keeps, covered, in the refrigerator for several days. Stir well before using.

Yield: 8 to 10 slices

Autumn Pumpkin Pancakes

	Nonstick cooking spray
2	cups biscuit mix
2	tablespoons packed light brown sugar
2	teaspoons cinnamon
1	teaspoon allspice
1	(12-ounce) can evaporated milk
1/2	cup canned pumpkin
2	tablespoons vegetable oil
2	eggs
1	teaspoon vanilla extract

Coat a griddle with the cooking spray. Heat.

Combine the biscuit mix, sugar, cinnamon and allspice in a large mixer bowl. Add the evaporated milk, pumpkin, oil, eggs and vanilla. Beat until smooth.

Pour the batter by tablespoonfuls onto the griddle. Cook until the tops are bubbly and the edges dry. Turn. Cook until the bottoms are golden. Serve with butter and warm maple syrup.

Yield: 16 pancakes

Allspice

Pungent aromatic spice, whole or in powdered form. It is excellent in marinades, particularly in game marinade, or in curries.

Banana Brunch Cake

Nonstick cooking spray
6 ounces cream cheese, softened
1/3 cup sugar
3 cups plus 1 tablespoon flour
1 teaspoon nutmeg
3 eggs
1/2 cup butter, softened
1 1/2 cups sugar
1 teaspoon baking soda
3 tablespoons hot water
1 teaspoon baking powder
1/2 teaspoon salt
1 1/4 teaspoons cinnamon
1/3 cup orange juice
1 teaspoon vanilla extract
3 medium ripe bananas, mashed
1 cup chopped pecans
1 tablespoon melted butter
1 tablespoon sugar

Preheat the oven to 350 degrees. Coat a 10-inch tube or bundt pan with the cooking spray.

Combine the cream cheese, 1/3 cup sugar, 1 tablespoon of the flour and 1/2 teaspoon of the nutmeg in a medium bowl. Beat until smooth. Add 1 of the eggs, beating to mix.

Cream 1/2 cup softened butter in a large bowl, gradually adding 1 1/2 cups sugar. Beat well. Add the remaining 2 eggs, one at a time, beating well after each addition. Whisk the baking soda and water in a small measuring cup. Mix into the butter mixture.

Combine the remaining 3 cups flour, the baking powder, salt, remaining 1/2 teaspoon nutmeg and 1 teaspoon of the cinnamon in a bowl. Mix, alternating with the orange juice, into the butter mixture. Mix in the vanilla, bananas and pecans.

Spoon 1 1/2 cups into the tube pan. Spread the cream cheese mixture over the banana batter. Spoon the remaining banana batter over the cream cheese mixture.

Bake for 50 to 55 minutes or until a wooden pick inserted in the center comes out clean. Cool for 15 minutes in the pan. Remove to a wire rack to finish cooling.

Brush with the melted butter. Mix together 1 tablespoon sugar and the remaining 1/4 teaspoon cinnamon. Sprinkle over the brunch cake.

Yield: 12 to 16 servings

Chocolate Chip Coffee Cake

	Nonstick cooking spray	1	teaspoon baking soda
2	cups semisweet chocolate chips	1/2	teaspoon cinnamon
1/4	cup packed light brown sugar	1	cup sour cream
1	cup coarsely chopped walnuts	1/2	cup butter, softened
	or pecans	1	cup sugar
2	cups flour	2	eggs
1	teaspoon baking powder	1	teaspoon vanilla extract

Preheat the oven to 350 degrees. Coat a 9-inch springform pan with the cooking spray.

Combine the chocolate chips, brown sugar and walnuts in a small bowl. Combine the flour, baking powder, baking soda and cinnamon in a medium bowl. Cream the sour cream, butter, sugar and eggs in a large bowl until blended. Mix in the vanilla. Add the flour mixture, beating until thoroughly combined.

Layer the batter and chocolate chip mixture, 1/2 at a time, in the springform pan, ending with the chocolate chip mixture. Bake for 40 to 45 minutes or until a wooden pick inserted in the center comes out clean.

Yield: 10 to 12 servings

Cinnamon Swirl Bread

For bread machine lovers! Freezes well.

Cinnamon Bread
1 cup milk
3 tablespoons butter
1 egg or $^1/_4$ cup egg substitute
$1^1/_2$ teaspoons salt
3 tablespoons sugar
2 tablespoons powdered milk
3 cups bread flour
$^3/_4$ teaspoon cinnamon

$2^1/_2$ teaspoons yeast
$^1/_2$ cup chocolate chips
$^1/_2$ cup chopped pecans

Chocolate Glaze
$^1/_4$ cup chocolate chips
1 tablespoon butter or margarine
$^1/_3$ cup confectioners' sugar
3 to 4 teaspoons water

For the cake, place the milk, butter, egg, salt, sugar, powdered milk, flour, cinnamon and yeast, in the order given, in the loaf pan of an electric bread machine. Set to the mix cycle.

When the timer indicates, add the chocolate chips and pecans. Bake until the bread tests done. Remove from the pan and cool on a wire rack.

For the glaze, melt the chocolate chips and butter in a small saucepan. Remove from the heat. Stir in the confectioners' sugar and water. Drizzle the warm glaze over the cooled bread.

Yield: 12 servings

Glazed Lemon Zucchini Bread

The lemon glaze adds a nice twist to this old standby.

Zucchini Bread
Nonstick cooking spray
1¹/₂ cups sifted flour
1¹/₂ teaspoons baking powder
¹/₄ teaspoon salt
¹/₃ cup margarine
1 cup sugar
Grated peel of 1 large lemon

²/₃ cup shredded zucchini
2 eggs
¹/₂ cup milk
¹/₂ cup finely chopped pecans

Lemon Glaze
¹/₃ cup sugar
Juice of 1 large lemon

Preheat the oven to 350 degrees. Coat a 3x9-inch loaf pan with the cooking spray.

For the bread, sift the flour, baking powder and salt into a medium bowl. Beat the margarine, sugar and lemon peel in another medium bowl until well blended. Mix in the zucchini. Add the eggs, one at a time, beating well after each addition. Mix in the flour mixture, alternating with the milk and ending with the flour. Fold in the pecans.

Spoon into the loaf pan. Bake for 45 to 50 minutes or until the bread pulls away from the sides of the pan and the top springs back when lightly touched. Place the loaf pan on a wire rack. Pierce the top of the warm bread, using a wooden pick.

For the glaze, combine the sugar and lemon juice in a small bowl. Pour evenly over the warm loaf. Let cool to room temperature. Loosen around the edges with a spatula. Turn out.

Yield: 8 servings

By The Hearth

As the evening air begins to chill, coming home to the glow of a fireplace warms the body and spirit. These soups and chilis, with their hearty ingredients, will restore home to your very soul.

**Designers
Phyllis Tomkins
and
Alice Tompkins**

**Photographer
Leland Lee**

**Pasadena Showcase
House of Design**

Chilled Peach Soup

1	quart frozen peaches, thawed	1/4	cup lemon juice
3/4	cup sour cream	1/4	cup dry sherry
3/4	cup pineapple juice		Fresh mint sprigs
1	cup orange juice		

Drain the peaches, reserving 1/2 cup of the juice. Combine the peaches and sour cream in a blender jar. Process until blended. Add the reserved peach juice, the pineapple, orange, and lemon juices, and the sherry. Process until blended, and strain.

Chill in the refrigerator for at least 30 minutes. Ladle into individual soup bowls. Garnish each serving with several mint sprigs.

Yield: 6 servings

Lemon Mango Soup

4	ripe mangoes, peeled, coarsely chopped		Zest of 2 lemons
	Juice of 2 lemons	1	pint raspberries
1	cup whipping cream		Fresh mint sprigs

Place the mangoes and lemon juice in a food processor bowl. Process until puréed. Pour 2 cups of the purée into a container. Chill, covered, until ready to use. Add the cream to the remaining purée. Process until blended.

Transfer the remaining mango mixture to a bowl. Add 3/4 of the lemon zest; mix well. Chill, covered, for 4 hours.

Ladle the mango mixture into individual soup bowls. Top each serving with a swirl of the reserved purée. Sprinkle the remaining lemon zest over each serving. Top with 3 or 4 raspberries and a mint sprig.

Yield: 4 servings

Light and Lively Gazpacho

Refreshing and delicious with a bite.

1	(30-ounce) can diced tomatoes		2	red bell peppers, diced
1	(46-ounce) can tomato juice		1	cucumber, peeled, seeded, diced
1	cup red wine vinegar		3	to 4 ribs celery, diced
1/4	cup olive oil		1	medium red onion, minced
3	tablespoons Worcestershire sauce			Salt to taste
				Tabasco sauce to taste
1	teaspoon freshly ground pepper		1	avocado, sliced
3	to 4 cloves garlic, minced			

Combine the tomatoes, tomato juice, vinegar, oil, Worcestershire sauce, pepper, garlic, bell peppers, cucumber, celery and onion in a large bowl. Season with the salt and Tabasco sauce. Stir gently until mixed.

Chill, covered, in the refrigerator for 3 to 4 hours. Ladle into individual soup bowls.

Garnish with avocado slices.

Yield: 12 servings

Cream of Carrot Soup

This beautiful golden soup makes a perfect first course.

1/4	cup unsalted butter	16	small carrots, sliced
1/4	cup flour	1	cup whipping cream
5	cups chicken stock or		Salt and white pepper to taste
	3 3/4 cups chicken broth plus		Minced parsley
	1 1/4 cups water	6	carrot curls

Melt the butter in a large saucepan over medium heat. Stir in the flour. Cook for 3 to 4 minutes. Stir in the chicken stock and carrots.

Bring to a boil over high heat. Reduce the heat. Simmer, covered, for 50 minutes. Let cool slightly.

Pour into a food processor bowl; process until puréed. Return the mixture to the saucepan. Stir in the cream. Season with the salt and pepper.

Simmer, uncovered, for 15 minutes. Ladle into individual soup bowls. Top each serving with the parsley and a carrot curl.

Yield: 6 servings

French Onion Soup

Please everyone at your table with almost no effort.

3	large yellow or white onions	1	teaspoon salt
1/2	cup unsalted butter	1/2	teaspoon freshly ground pepper
3	tablespoons flour	1	dried baguette, cut into 6 slices
8	cups beef stock	2	cups shredded Gruyère cheese

Cut the onions into halves lengthwise. Place in a food processor container. Process until chopped.

Melt the butter in a saucepan over medium heat. Add the onions; sauté until tender. Add the flour; cook for 5 minutes or until the onions are browned, stirring frequently. Stir in the stock, salt and pepper.

Bring the mixture to a boil over high heat. Reduce the heat to medium. Simmer, covered, for 15 minutes or until the onions are translucent.

Ladle into broiler-safe soup bowls; top each with 1 bread slice. Sprinkle the cheese over the bread. Broil until lightly browned.

Yield: 6 servings

Beautiful Bowls

Instead of serving your soup in a bowl, try serving it in a bread bowl. For each bowl, start with a round loaf of bread and cut a lid, leaving approximately a 1-inch edge. Hollow out and brush the inside of the loaf and lid with olive oil. Place on a baking sheet and bake at 350 degrees for 10 to 12 minutes.

The bread that was removed can be used as croutons.

Try this tip with a heavy soup such as the Potato and Corn Chowder on page 76.

Designers
Phyllis Tomkins
and
Alice Tompkins

Photographer
Cameron
Carothers

Previous Pages

**Designer
Robin Dorman**

**Photographer
Weldon Brewster**

Butternut Squash Soup

3	tablespoons butter
1	(2-pound) butternut squash, seeded, cut into 8 pieces
1	pound parsnips, cut into 2-inch slices
1/4	cup water
1	onion, thinly sliced
2	teaspoons chopped fresh thyme, or 3/4 teaspoon dried
4	cups chicken broth
1	cup half-and-half
	Salt and pepper to taste

Preheat the oven to 375 degrees. Butter a large roasting pan with 1 tablespoon of the butter. Arrange the squash skin side down and parsnips in the pan; add the water. Cover with foil. Bake for 50 minutes or until the vegetables are very tender. Let cool. Melt the remaining 2 tablespoons butter in a large heavy skillet over medium-low heat. Add the onion and thyme. Sauté for 10 minutes or until the onion is tender and golden. Remove from the heat.

Combine the squash, parsnips and onion in a food processor bowl. Process until puréed. Add the broth; process until blended. Pour the mixture into a large heavy saucepan. Whisk in the half-and-half. Bring to a simmer. Season with the salt and pepper.

Hint: May be made ahead and stored, covered, in the refrigerator for 1 day.

Yield: 6 servings

Vegetable Chili

A heartwarming main dish.

2	(28-ounce) cans peeled plum tomatoes	1	tablespoon tomato paste
1/4	cup olive oil	1	tablespoon brown sugar
4	medium onions, chopped	2	teaspoons dried oregano
4	medium carrots, cut into 1/2-inch slices	1	teaspoon fennel seeds
2	tablespoons minced garlic	2	medium yellow squash, seeded, cut into 1/2-inch cubes
2	tablespoons chili powder	2	medium zucchini, cut into 1/2-inch cubes
2	tablespoons ground cumin	1	(15 1/2-ounce) can garbanzo beans
8	ounces red new potatoes, cut into 1/2-inch cubes	1/2	cup chopped parsley
1	each red, green and yellow bell peppers, cut into 1/2-inch pieces		Salt and pepper to taste
		2	tablespoons fresh lemon juice

Chop the plum tomatoes, reserving the juice. Warm the oil in a large heavy saucepan over medium heat for 1 minute. Add the onions and carrots. Cook for 8 minutes, stirring constantly. Add the garlic. Cook for 2 minutes, stirring often. Reduce the heat to low.

Stir in the chili powder and cumin. Cook for 1 minute. Stir in the potatoes, bell peppers, undrained chopped tomatoes, tomato paste, brown sugar, oregano and fennel seeds. Bring to a boil. Reduce the heat to medium. Simmer, partially covered, for 25 minutes, stirring occasionally.

Stir in the squash, zucchini, beans and parsley. Season with the salt and pepper. Simmer, uncovered, for 20 minutes or until the vegetables are tender, stirring occasionally. Stir in the lemon juice.

Hint: To save a bit of time, buy pre-minced garlic in a jar at your grocery store.

Yield: 10 servings

White Chicken Chili

4   quarts water
1½   cups cream sherry
1   teaspoon salt
2   pounds boneless, skinless
     chicken breasts
¼   cup butter or margarine
1   large onion, chopped
1   clove garlic, finely chopped
2   tablespoons chopped fresh
     cilantro

1   tablespoon chopped fresh basil,
     or ½ tablespoon dried
¼   teaspoon chili powder
¼   teaspoon ground cloves
2   (16-ounce) cans Great
     Northern white beans
2   medium tomatoes, chopped
     Chopped cilantro
     Sour cream
     Blue corn tortilla chips

Combine the water, sherry, salt and chicken in a stockpot. Bring to a boil over high heat. Reduce the heat to medium. Simmer, covered, for 20 minutes or until the chicken is cooked through. Remove the chicken to a platter. Chill, covered with plastic wrap, for 4 hours. Chill the stock, covered, in the refrigerator for 4 hours or until the fat congeals on the surface. Skim off the fat.

Cut the chicken into bite-size pieces. Melt the butter in a large heavy saucepan over medium heat. Add the onion and garlic. Cook until tender. Stir in 3 cups stock, the chicken, cilantro, basil, chili powder, cloves and beans. Bring to a boil. Reduce the heat to medium. Simmer, covered, for about 1 hour, stirring occasionally.

Ladle into individual soup bowls. Top each serving with the tomatoes, cilantro and sour cream. Serve with the tortilla chips.

Yield: 10 servings

Hearty Sierra Chili

1	pound ground lamb	1	(28-ounce) can chopped
1	pound ground pork		tomatoes
1	pound ground beef	2	(16-ounce) cans pinto beans
1	teaspoon cumin	1	cup beer
3	tablespoons chili powder	1	teaspoon salt
2	teaspoons coriander	1	teaspoon pepper
1	green bell pepper, chopped		Chopped onions
6	cloves garlic, chopped		Shredded Cheddar cheese
1	large onion, chopped		Chopped green chiles
1	(16-ounce) can tomato sauce		

Brown the lamb, pork and beef in a large skillet, stirring until crumbly and no longer pink; drain. Remove to a stockpot. Stir in the cumin, chili powder, coriander, bell pepper, garlic, onion, tomato sauce, chopped tomatoes, beans, beer, salt and pepper. Cover the pot.

Bring the mixture to a boil. Turn the heat to low. Simmer, covered, for 3 hours, stirring occasionally. Ladle into individual soup bowls. Top each serving with the onions, cheese and chiles.

Yield: 12 servings

Oregano

A staple, savory herb in Italian, Spanish, Greek, and Mexican cuisines. It is very good in dishes with a tomato foundation, especially in combination with basil.

Spicy Jambalaya

1/4	cup unsalted butter
1	pound chorizo or other spicy sausage, cut into 1/4-inch slices
8	ounces boneless, skinless chicken breast, cut into 1/2-inch cubes
1	pound shrimp, peeled, deveined, tails removed
3	tomatoes, chopped
1	each large red and green bell peppers, chopped
4	cloves garlic, chopped
1	large red onion, chopped
1	quart chicken broth
1 1/2	cups white rice
1/8	teaspoon ground cloves
1	teaspoon dried basil
1	teaspoon dried oregano
1	teaspoon dried thyme
1	teaspoon dried rosemary
1	bay leaf
	Dash of red wine
	Tabasco sauce to taste
	Salt and pepper to taste

Melt the butter in a large stockpot over medium heat. Add the sausage and chicken. Cook for 5 minutes or until cooked through. Stir in the shrimp. Cook until the shrimp turn pink. Stir in the tomatoes, bell peppers, garlic and onion. Cook, covered, until the vegetables are tender.

Pour in the stock. Bring to a boil over high heat. Add the rice, cloves, basil, oregano, thyme, rosemary, bay leaf and wine. Season with the Tabasco sauce, salt and pepper. Cook, uncovered, over medium-low heat for 45 minutes or until the rice is tender. Discard the bay leaf. Serve in individual soup bowls with additional Tabasco sauce to taste.

Yield: 10 servings

Lentil Soup with Andouille Sausage

The andouille sausage and fennel give this soup a remarkable flavor.

1 1/2 cups dried lentils
4 1/2 cups chicken broth
4 1/2 cups beef broth
2   teaspoons fennel seeds
2   tablespoons olive oil
1/3 cup chopped celery
1/3 cup chopped carrot
1/3 cup chopped onion
1   clove garlic, minced
8   ounces andouille sausage, halved lengthwise, cut into 1/2-inch slices
2   teaspoons dried thyme
1/2 teaspoon Creole seasoning
    Salt and pepper to taste

Rinse and sort the lentils. Combine the chicken broth, beef broth and lentils in a stockpot. Bring to a boil over high heat. Reduce the heat to medium. Simmer, covered, for 30 minutes.

Spread the fennel in a medium skillet. Sauté over medium heat for 2 minutes or until the seeds are golden. Remove the seeds to a small bowl.

Warm the oil in the same skillet over medium heat. Add the celery, carrot, onion and garlic. Sauté for 5 minutes or until the onion is translucent and the celery and carrot are tender.

Stir the fennel seeds, vegetables, sausage, thyme and Creole seasoning into the broth and lentil mixture. Simmer, covered, for 45 minutes or until the lentils are very tender, stirring occasionally. Season with the salt and pepper.

Hint: May be made ahead and stored, covered, in the refrigerator for 1 day. May substitute bratwurst, kielbasa or smoked Hungarian sausage for the andouille.

Yield: 6 servings

Fennel

Once called the "meetin' seed" by the Puritans, who nibbled on it during meetings, fennel seed is originally from India. It has a unique licorice flavor and is used to enhance Italian sausage, pork, poultry, and seafood recipes.

In The Garden

Step into our garden and find ways to refresh your salads with new dressings and different combinations of ingredients . . . a sure way to help your meal make a splash!

**Designer
Lauren Elia**

**Photographer
Cameron
Carothers**

A Palate for Pansies

At the California Institute of Technology, legend has it that Mrs. Albert Einstein once introduced a group of luncheon attendees at The Athenaeum, the school's exclusive club, to the taste of flowers. Evidently, Mrs. Einstein had failing eyesight and mistook a corsage laid near her plate to be part of her salad. When she took a forkful of her flowers and ate them, the luncheon attendees followed suit in order not to offend their famous guest.

See page 105 for a list of edible flowers.

Designer
Diana Clark

Photographer
Cameron
Carothers

Quick and Easy Salad with Spring Greens and Gorgonzola

Always a favorite!

1 (5-ounce) bag spring greens
¹/₄ cup pine nuts, toasted
¹/₃ cup dried cranberries
¹/₂ cup crumbled Gorgonzola cheese
   Freshly ground pepper
¹/₄ to ¹/₂ cup balsamic vinaigrette

Combine the greens, nuts, cranberries and cheese in a large salad bowl.

Add the pepper and vinaigrette, and toss to coat.

Yield: 4 servings

Wedding Shower Chicken Salad

Perfect for a spring wedding or baby shower.

Ginger Dressing
3/4	cup mayonnaise
1	teaspoon minced candied ginger
2	tablespoons red wine vinegar
1	tablespoon soy sauce
2	tablespoons minced onion
1/2	teaspoon curry powder

Chicken Salad
8	chilled cooked boneless, skinless chicken breasts, cut into bite-size pieces
1/2	cup drained sliced water chestnuts
1/2	cup chopped pecans
1/2	cup halved seedless green grapes
1/4	cup chopped celery
1	(8-ounce) can pineapple chunks, drained

For the dressing, whisk the mayonnaise, ginger, vinegar, soy sauce, onion and curry powder in a small bowl.

For the salad, combine the chicken, water chestnuts, pecans, grapes, celery and pineapple in a large bowl. Pour in the dressing, and toss to coat. Chill, covered, in the refrigerator for 2 to 3 hours before serving.

Serve with croissants, on lettuce or in pineapple halves.

Yield: 8 servings

Turkey Salad with a Twist

Make this wonderful, lean salad with your Thanksgiving leftovers.

Mustard Dressing
1   cup plain nonfat
     yogurt
1/2 cup Dijon mustard
1   tablespoon honey
     Salt and pepper to taste

Turkey Salad
1   head red leaf lettuce, torn
2   to 3 cups shredded oven-
     roasted turkey breast
1   cup dried cranberries
1/2 cup chopped walnuts, toasted

For the dressing, whisk the yogurt, mustard, honey, salt and pepper in a small bowl.

For the salad, combine the lettuce, turkey, cranberries and walnuts in a large bowl. Pour in the dressing, and toss to coat.

Yield: 4 servings

Marinated Garbanzo Bean Salad

A flavorful addition to your summer picnic table.

1/2 cup olive oil
1   cup finely minced onions
1   tablespoon thyme
1/2 cup finely chopped red bell
     pepper

1/2 cup raisins
2   cups canned garbanzo beans,
     rinsed, drained
1/2 teaspoon salt
1/2 cup white wine vinegar

Warm the olive oil in a saucepan over low heat. Add the onions and thyme. Cook, covered, for 25 minutes or until the onions are tender and slightly browned. Stir in the bell pepper. Cook for 5 minutes. Stir in the raisins and garbanzo beans. Cook for 5 minutes, stirring occasionally. Season with the salt.

Remove to a bowl, and pour the vinegar over the mixture. Let cool to room temperature. Chill, covered, in the refrigerator for 24 hours before serving. Serve at room temperature.

Yield: 6 servings

Black Bean and Corn Fiesta Salad

A beautiful and tasty salad.

Spicy Dressing
3/4   cup Italian salad dressing
3/4   teaspoon hot pepper sauce (optional)
1/2   teaspoon chili powder (optional)
1   tablespoon lemon juice
1   cup chopped fresh cilantro
1/2   teaspoon seasoned pepper

Bean and Corn Salad
1   (15-ounce) can black beans, rinsed, drained
1   (12-ounce) can whole kernel corn, drained
1   red bell pepper, finely chopped
1/2   cup chopped red onion
1   clove garlic, minced
1   medium tomato, chopped
1   jalapeño, seeded, finely chopped (optional)
1/2   bunch cilantro, chopped

For the dressing, combine the salad dressing, pepper sauce, chili powder, lemon juice, cilantro and seasoned pepper in a jar. Shake to mix well.

For the salad, combine the beans, corn, bell pepper, onion, garlic, tomato and jalapeño in a bowl. Pour the dressing over the salad. Stir gently to mix. Marinate, covered, in the refrigerator for at least 6 hours to blend flavors. Garnish with the cilantro before serving.

Yield: 8 servings

Edible Cactus

You can add south-of-the border flair to any meal with the addition of edible cacti. Gaining popularity in the U.S., cacti can be found in specialty markets. The pads of the Prickly Pear cactus can be used in salads, egg dishes, and soups, serving as a good source of Vitamins A, B, C and iron.

Designer Robin Dorman

Photographer Lori and Fred Stocker

Summer Salad

A wonderful blend of ingredients. You will want to serve this throughout the year!

Cider Vinaigrette

1	cup sugar
1	cup cider vinegar
1½	cups vegetable oil
	Pepper to taste

Pasta and Chicken Salad

12	ounces tricolor fusilli, cooked, drained
3	to 4 boneless, skinless chicken breasts, cooked, cut into bite-size pieces
2½	cups red seedless grapes, halved
½	(16-ounce) package frozen peas, thawed
4	cups torn spinach leaves
6	ribs celery, sliced
1	(13¾-ounce) can artichoke hearts, drained, chopped
1	large cucumber, peeled, cubed
3	green onions, sliced
	Avocado or orange slices (optional)

For the vinaigrette, combine the sugar and vinegar in a microwave-safe bowl. Microwave, tightly covered, on High for 2 minutes or until the sugar is dissolved. Stir in the oil and pepper. Shake or mix well. Chill, covered, in the refrigerator. Shake or mix well before using.

For the salad, combine the fusilli, chicken, grapes, peas, spinach, celery, artichokes, cucumber and green onions. Divide the salad among individual bowls. Drizzle the dressing over the salad. May be garnished with avocado or orange slices.

Hint: May be stored, covered, in the refrigerator for up to 5 days.

Yield: 10 servings

Edible Flowers

For a flowery touch, you can add any of the following edible flowers to your next salad:
Apple Blossom, Bee Balm, Calendula (Pot Marigold), Day Lily, Lavender, Lilac, Nasturtium, Pansies, Primrose, Rose, Snapdragon, Tulip, Violet.

Remember to:
- *Only eat the flower petals for most flowers.*
- *Always remove the pistils and stamens before eating.*
- *Do not eat flowers that have been sprayed with pesticides.*
- *Check any flowers you have not chosen yourself.*

Designer
Maxine White

Photographer
Weldon Brewster

White Rice Salad with Asparagus and Cucumber

Dijon Dill Dressing
2   tablespoons Dijon mustard
1   tablespoon sugar
1   tablespoon white wine
     vinegar
1/2 teaspoon dry mustard
2 1/2 tablespoons vegetable oil
1/4 cup chopped fresh dill

Rice Salad
1 3/4 cups water
1   cup long grain white rice
     Salt to taste
1   pound asparagus, cut into
     1-inch slices
1 1/2 cups diced English cucumber
3   green onions, chopped

For the dressing, whisk the Dijon mustard, sugar, vinegar and dry mustard in a small bowl. Drizzle in the oil, whisking constantly. Stir in the dill.

For the salad, bring the water to a boil in a large saucepan. Stir in the rice. Return to a boil. Reduce the heat to low. Cook, covered, for 20 minutes or until the rice is tender and the water is absorbed. Fluff with a fork. Remove to a large bowl. Let cool to room temperature.

Fill a saucepan with salted water. Bring to a boil. Add the asparagus. Reduce the heat to low. Cook, covered, for 2 minutes or until tender-crisp; drain. Cool under cold running water; drain well.

Add the asparagus, cucumber and green onions to the rice. Pour in the dressing, and toss to coat.

Hint: The dressing and salad may be made ahead and stored, separately and covered, in the refrigerator for up to 1 day.

Yield: 8 servings

The Best Chinese Chicken Salad

Sesame Ginger Dressing
1/2 cup rice wine vinegar
1/3 cup sugar
1 tablespoon soy sauce
1 1/2 tablespoons grated gingerroot
1 tablespoon sesame oil
1 teaspoon salt

Chicken Salad
1 pound boneless, skinless chicken breasts
1/2 cup coarsely chopped gingerroot
1/2 onion, coarsely chopped
1 teaspoon garlic salt

1/2 teaspoon pepper
2 cups shredded iceberg lettuce
1 small head leaf lettuce, torn
3/4 cup diagonally sliced celery
1/3 cup sliced green onions
1 carrot, peeled, julienned
1 small green bell pepper, cut into 1/8-inch slices
1 (6-ounce) package Maifun noodles, cooked, chopped
1 bunch cilantro, chopped
1 tablespoon sesame seeds, toasted
1/3 pound won ton skins, cut into 1/4-inch strips, deep fried

For the dressing, whisk the vinegar, sugar, soy sauce, gingerroot, oil and salt in a small bowl. Chill, covered, in the refrigerator until ready to use.

For the salad, combine the chicken, gingerroot, onion, garlic salt and pepper in a saucepan. Pour in enough water to cover the chicken. Bring to a boil. Simmer, covered, for 1 hour or until cooked through. Let cool in the broth. Shred the chicken.

Combine the chicken, iceberg and leaf lettuces, celery, green onions, carrot, bell pepper, noodles, cilantro, sesame seeds and won ton strips in a large bowl. Pour in the dressing, and toss to coat.

Yield: 6 servings

Tortilla Shrimp Salad

Lime Dressing

3   tablespoons lime juice
1/2 small fresh red chile, seeded, minced
1/4 teaspoon salt
2   tablespoons vegetable oil

Tortilla Chips

Vegetable oil for frying
6   (8-inch) corn or flour tortillas, quartered

Shrimp and Goat Cheese Salad

6   cups spring greens
1   ripe mango, peeled, cut into 1-inch cubes
1   cup cooked black beans, rinsed
1/2 small red onion, thinly sliced
1   pound cooked peeled, deveined shrimp
1/4 cup mild goat cheese, crumbled

For the dressing, combine the lime juice, chile, salt and vegetable oil in a small bowl.

For the chips, heat 1/8 inch vegetable oil in a large skillet over moderately high heat until almost smoking. Add as many tortilla quarters as will fit without overlapping. Fry for 4 minutes or until crisp and golden on both sides turning once. Remove the chips to paper towels; drain. Repeat the process until all the tortilla quarters have been cooked.

For the salad, toss the greens and 1 1/2 tablespoons of the dressing in a bowl. Mound the greens on a large platter. Combine the mango, beans, onion and 3 tablespoons of the dressing in a medium bowl, and toss to coat. Arrange over the greens. Top with the shrimp and cheese. Arrange the tortilla chips around the platter.

Yield: 4 servings

Basil Buttermilk Dressing

Wonderful with fresh tomatoes.

2   cups loosely packed basil
   leaves, chopped
3/4 cup buttermilk
2   green onions, chopped

3/4 teaspoon salt
3/4 cup mayonnaise
1/4 teaspoon pepper

Whisk the basil, buttermilk, green onions, salt, mayonnaise and pepper in a small bowl.

May be drizzled over tomatoes or salad greens.

Yield: 1¼ cups

Orange Poppy Seed Dressing

Serve with a salad of spinach, red onion slices, toasted pecan halves and cubed cantaloupe.

3   tablespoons sugar
1½ teaspoons grated orange peel
2   tablespoons orange juice
2   tablespoons vinegar
   Dash of pepper

1   tablespoon finely chopped
   onion
1/3 cup vegetable oil
1   teaspoon poppy seeds

Combine the sugar, orange peel, orange juice, vinegar, pepper and onion in a food processor bowl or blender jar. Process until combined.

Add the oil in a fine stream, processing constantly at high speed until smooth and thick. Stir in the poppy seeds.

Chill, covered, in the refrigerator for up to 1 week. Shake or stir before using.

Yield: ¾ cup

Patterns &
Pasta

*Dining "al fresco," or in the
fresh air, adds a touch of
novelty to your meal by
providing an exquisite
outdoor backdrop for a
change of scene. For a
different view of pasta, the
recipes in this chapter
promise you fresh and
colorful dining, both indoors
and outdoors.*

**Designer
Judy Kenyon
Burness**

**Photographer
Cameron
Carothers**

Linguini with Lemon Alfredo Sauce

Easy, easy, easy! Add cubed cooked chicken for a heartier meal.

Salt to taste
1 (9-ounce) package fresh linguini
3/4 cup whipping cream
1 tablespoon butter

3 tablespoons lemon juice
1 tablespoon grated lemon peel
1/2 cup grated Parmesan cheese
Pepper to taste

Bring salted water to a boil in a saucepan over high heat. Add the linguini. Cook, uncovered, until al dente. Drain, reserving 1/2 cup cooking water.

Combine the cream and butter in a large heavy skillet. Bring to a simmer over medium-high heat. Stir in the lemon juice and peel.

Add the pasta; toss to coat, adding the reserved water as needed to thin the sauce to the desired consistency. Add the cheese, and toss to coat. Season with the salt and pepper.

Yield: 4 servings

Pasta with Creamy Mushroom Sauce

Look for dried wild mushrooms at most supermarkets; they lend a wonderful richness to this dish, which is great with garlic bread.

1	ounce dried mushrooms (porcini, morels or shiitake)	1/4	cup thinly sliced green onions
1	cup boiling water	1	teaspoon lemon juice
1/2	cup dry white wine		Salt and pepper to taste
1/2	cup whipping cream	8	ounces fresh or dried angel hair pasta
3/4	teaspoon dried tarragon		

Place the mushrooms in a small bowl. Pour in the water. Let stand, covered, for 15 minutes or until the mushrooms soften. Remove the mushrooms to a work surface; reserve the soaking liquid. Coarsely chop the mushrooms; discard tough stems.

Combine the wine and mushrooms in a large heavy skillet. Bring to a boil. Cook for 2 minutes or until the wine is reduced to about 1/4 cup. Stir in the cream and tarragon. Pour in the reserved soaking liquid slowly, leaving the sediment in the bottom of the bowl. Boil for 5 minutes or until the sauce is thick enough to coat a spoon. Stir in the green onions and lemon juice. Season with the salt and pepper.

Bring salted water to a boil in a large saucepan over high heat. Add the angel hair pasta. Cook until al dente; drain. Add the pasta to the sauce, and toss gently to coat.

Hint: The recipe may be doubled.

Yield: 2 servings

Red Pepper Pasta

3   large red bell peppers, cut into thin strips
2   tablespoons minced garlic
8   tablespoons olive oil
    Salt and pepper to taste
1½ pounds linguini

1½ cups chopped onions
¾   cup coarsely chopped walnuts, toasted
⅓   cup chopped fresh parsley
1½ cups grated Parmesan cheese

Combine the bell peppers, garlic and 6½ tablespoons of the oil in a large bowl. Season with the salt and pepper. Marinate, covered, at room temperature for 2 hours.

Fill a large pot with salted water and bring to a boil over high heat. Add the linguini. Cook until al dente; drain.

Warm the remaining 1½ tablespoons oil in a large heavy skillet over medium-high heat. Add the onions. Sauté for 6 minutes or until tender and brown. Stir in the bell pepper mixture. Sauté for 4 minutes. Add the pasta; toss to coat. Remove to a serving bowl. Add the walnuts, parsley and Parmesan cheese; toss to coat.

Hint: The bell peppers may be marinated in a covered container in the refrigerator for up to 12 hours. Pine nuts may be substituted for the walnuts.

Yield: 6 servings

Roasted Pepper Pasta Sauce

A nice change from the usual tomato sauce.

1	small onion	2	tablespoons sugar
1	medium carrot	1	teaspoon freshly ground pepper
2	to 3 cloves garlic	1	teaspoon salt
1/4	cup olive oil	1	(6-ounce) can tomato sauce
6	medium tomatoes, chopped	1	(10-ounce) can chicken broth
2	to 3 tablespoons minced fresh basil	1	medium to large yellow bell pepper
2	teaspoons dried oregano		

Combine the onion, carrot and garlic in a food processor bowl. Process until puréed.

Warm the oil in a large skillet over medium-high heat. Add the onion and carrot mixture. Cook for 5 to 10 minutes, being careful not to brown the mixture. Stir in the tomatoes, basil, oregano, sugar, pepper, salt, tomato sauce and broth. Bring to a boil over high heat. Reduce the heat to low and simmer for 15 minutes.

To roast the pepper, skewer it with a long-handled fork, and hold over the open flame of a gas stove or place under a broiler. Cook until the skin is charred on all sides, turning as necessary. Place in a bowl covered with plastic wrap. Let stand for 5 minutes or until cool enough to handle. Rinse under cool running water, wiping away the blackened skin. Core the pepper and rinse away the seeds. Place in a food processor bowl. Process until puréed.

Stir into the tomato mixture. Simmer for 5 to 10 minutes. Serve over pasta.

Yield: 4 servings

Wine Pronunciations

Frascati	*Fras-cah-tee*
Fendant	*Fahn-dawn*
Vouvray	*Voo-vray*
Chablis	*Shab-lee*
Pinot Blanc	*Pee-no Blawn*
Verdicchio	*Ver-deek-ee-o*
Sancerre	*Sahn-sehr*
Soave	*So-ah-veh*
Beaujolais	*Bo-sho-lay*
Barbera	*Bar-bear-ah*
Lambrusco	*Lom-bruce-co*
Lirac	*Lee-rack*
Barolo	*Bah-ro-lo*
Cote Rotie	*Coat Ro-tee*
Hermitage	*Air-me-tahz*
Merlot	*Mair-lo*
Syrah	*Sir-rah*

**Designer
Cynthia
Bennett**

**Photographer
Weldon
Brewster**

Penne with Spicy Vodka Sauce

4	tablespoons extra-virgin olive oil		Salt to taste	
4	cloves garlic, minced	1	pound penne	
1/2	teaspoon crushed red pepper flakes	2	tablespoons vodka	
3/4	teaspoon salt	1/2	cup whipping cream	
1	(28-ounce) can crushed tomatoes	1/4	cup chopped fresh flat-leaf parsley	

Warm the oil in a large skillet over medium heat. Add the garlic and red pepper. Cook until the garlic is golden, stirring constantly. Stir in 3/4 teaspoon salt and tomatoes. Bring to a boil. Reduce the heat to medium. Simmer for 15 minutes.

Fill a large pot with salted water, and bring to a boil over high heat. Add the penne. Cook until al dente; drain. Return to the pot. Stir the vodka and cream into the tomato mixture. Bring to a boil. Stir the tomato and cream mixture into the penne. Cook for 1 minute. Add the parsley, and toss to coat.

Yield: 4 servings

Herbed Ricotta and Rotelle

Can be prepared in 45 minutes or less.

15	ounces low-fat ricotta cheese	1/4	cup chopped fresh chives or green onions
2/3	cup skim milk	1/4	cup chopped fresh parsley
1/2	cup grated Parmesan cheese		Salt to taste
2	teaspoons olive oil	12	ounces rotelle or fusilli
1	cup chopped onion		Pepper to taste
2	cloves garlic, chopped		
1/4	to 1/2 cup chopped fresh basil		

Combine the ricotta cheese, skim milk and Parmesan cheese in a food processor bowl. Process until blended.

Warm the oil in a large heavy skillet over medium heat. Add the onion. Sauté for 5 minutes or until the onion begins to brown. Add the garlic. Sautè for 2 minutes. Stir in the ricotta mixture, the basil, chives and parsley. Cook for 5 minutes or until heated through.

Fill a large pot with salted water, and bring to a boil over high heat. Add the rotelle. Cook until al dente; drain. Add the rotelle to the ricotta mixture, and toss to coat. Season with the salt and pepper.

Hint: May add cooked shrimp or cubed cooked chicken for variety.

Yield: 4 servings

Classic Lasagna

The flavor improves if this dish is assembled a day ahead; store in the refrigerator until ready to use. Recipe can easily be halved.

3	tablespoons olive oil	1	teaspoon sugar
2	medium onions, chopped	1	teaspoon dried oregano
2	cloves garlic, crushed		Salt and pepper to taste
2	pounds Italian sausage, thinly sliced	8	ounces lasagna noodles
1½	pounds ground beef	8	ounces mozzarella cheese, sliced
2	(6-ounce) cans tomato paste	12	ounces ricotta cheese
1	(28-ounce) can Italian plum tomatoes	½	cup grated Parmesan cheese

Warm 2 tablespoons of the oil in a skillet over medium heat. Add the onions and garlic. Sauté until the onions are soft. Stir in the sausage and beef. Cook until browned and crumbly, stirring frequently; drain. Stir in the tomato paste, plum tomatoes, sugar and oregano. Season with the salt and pepper. Simmer, covered, for at least 20 minutes.

Fill a large pot with salted water and the remaining 1 tablespoon oil; bring to a boil over high heat. Add the noodles. Cook until al dente; drain. Rinse under cool running water.

Preheat the oven to 375 degrees. Layer the noodles, mozzarella cheese, ricotta cheese and the tomato mixture, ½ at a time, in a rectangular 3-quart casserole, ending with the tomato mixture. Sprinkle the Parmesan cheese over the top. Bake for 25 minutes.

Yield: 12 servings

Linguini with Chicken and Walnuts

2	tablespoons olive oil	1/4	teaspoon cayenne
3	skinless, boneless chicken breasts halves, cut into 3/4-inch pieces	2/3	cup chopped toasted walnuts
		1/2	cup frozen green peas
		2/3	cup whipping cream
	Salt and pepper to taste	1/2	cup reduced-sodium chicken broth
1	medium red bell pepper, diced		
1	small onion, chopped	8	ounces linguini
1/2	teaspoon ground nutmeg	1/3	cup grated Parmesan cheese

Warm the oil in a large heavy skillet over high heat. Season the chicken with salt and pepper. Place the chicken in the skillet. Sauté for 5 minutes or until light brown and cooked through. Remove the chicken to a plate.

Combine the bell pepper, onion, nutmeg and cayenne in the same skillet. Sauté for 4 minutes or until the pepper begins to soften. Stir in 1/3 cup of the walnuts and the peas. Stir in the cream and broth. Boil, uncovered, for 6 minutes or until thickened to the consistency of a sauce, stirring constantly.

Fill a large pot with salted water, and bring to a boil over high heat. Add the linguini. Cook until al dente; drain. Add the linguini to the cream mixture. Stir in the remaining 1/3 cup walnuts and chicken; toss to distribute. Cook until heated through. Season with the salt and pepper. Remove to a serving bowl. Sprinkle the Parmesan cheese over the linguini and sauce.

Yield: 4 servings

Herbs

Use fresh whole herbs when possible. When fresh herbs are not available, use whole dried herbs that can be crushed just while adding. Store herbs in airtight containers away from the heat of the stove. Fresh herbs may be layered between paper towels and dried in the microwave on High for 2 minutes or until dry.

**Designer
Ann Fletcher**

**Photographer
Cameron
Carothers**

Penne with Italian Sausage and Mascarpone

12	ounces hot Italian sausage, casing removed	2	cups frozen green peas
12	ounces sweet (mild) Italian sausage, casing removed	2/3	cup mascarpone cheese
1	cup chopped onion		Salt to taste
1 1/4	cups whipping cream	1	pound penne
3/4	cup reduced-sodium chicken broth	3/4	cup grated Parmesan cheese
			Pepper to taste

Brown the sausages in a large heavy saucepan over high heat for 12 minutes or until cooked through, stirring to crumble. Remove to a bowl, using a slotted spoon. Drain the pan, reserving 1 tablespoon drippings in the pan.

Stir in the onion. Sauté for 6 minutes or until golden. Stir in the cream. Boil for 5 minutes. Stir in the broth. Boil for 8 minutes or until reduced to the consistency of a sauce, stirring occasionally. Return the sausage to the pan. Bring to a simmer over medium heat. Stir in the peas and mascarpone. Simmer, uncovered, for 6 minutes or until the peas are tender.

Fill a large pot with salted water, and bring to a boil over high heat. Add the penne. Cook until al dente; drain. Add to the sauce, and toss to coat. Add the Parmesan cheese; toss to distribute. Season with the salt and pepper.

Hint: If mascarpone, an Italian cream cheese, is unavailable, substitute a mixture of 6 tablespoons cream cheese and 5 tablespoons whipping cream.

Yield: 6 servings

Baked Ziti with Spinach and Tomatoes

12	ounces hot Italian sausage, casing removed		Vegetable oil
1	medium onion, chopped	10	ounces ziti or penne
3	large cloves garlic, chopped	1	(6-ounce) package ready-to-use spinach leaves
1	(28-ounce) can diced tomatoes	8	ounces mozzarella cheese, shredded
1/2	cup pesto sauce		
	Salt and pepper to taste	1	cup grated Parmesan cheese

Warm a large heavy saucepan over medium-high heat. Combine the sausage, onion and garlic in the pan. Sauté for 10 minutes or until the sausage is cooked through, stirring to crumble; drain. Stir in the undrained tomatoes. Simmer for 10 minutes or until the sauce thickens slightly, stirring occasionally. Stir in the pesto. Season with the salt and pepper.

Preheat the oven to 375 degrees. Coat a 9x13-inch baking dish with a small amount of the oil.

Fill a large pot with salted water, and bring to a boil over high heat. Add the ziti. Cook until al dente; drain. Combine the ziti, spinach, mozzarella cheese and 1/3 cup of the Parmesan cheese in a large bowl. Stir in the tomato mixture. Remove to the baking dish. Sprinkle the remaining 2/3 cup Parmesan cheese over the ziti mixture.

Bake for 30 minutes or until the sauce bubbles and the cheese melts.

Yield: 4 servings

Salmon Primavera over Whole Wheat Fettuccini

This is great for entertaining, and very healthy, too.

1	cup water	1	cup quartered mushrooms
12	ounces salmon fillet	1	red bell pepper, julienned
1/3	cup dry white wine	1 1/2	cups marinara sauce
	Salt to taste	1/3	cup low-fat buttermilk
10	ounces whole wheat fettuccini	2	tablespoons grated Parmesan
2	cups broccoli florets		cheese (optional)

Pour the water into a medium skillet. Add the salmon. Simmer, covered, over medium-high heat for 7 minutes or until the fish flakes easily when probed with a fork. Remove to a bowl. Pour in the wine.

Fill a large pot with salted water, and bring to a boil over high heat. Add the fettuccini. Cook until al dente; drain. Return the pasta to the pot; cover to keep warm.

Combine the broccoli, mushrooms and bell pepper in a steamer basket. Steam over boiling water for 3 to 4 minutes or until tender-crisp.

Combine the marinara sauce and buttermilk in a small saucepan. Cook over low heat until hot.

Arrange the fettuccini on a large platter. Drain the salmon. Flake into bite-size pieces, discarding skin and bones. Top the fettuccini with the vegetables, salmon and marinara mixture; toss to combine. Sprinkle with the Parmesan cheese.

Hint: Low-fat (1%) milk plus 1 teaspoon cider vinegar may be substituted for the buttermilk. Let the mixture stand for 10 minutes before using.

Yield: 6 servings

Asian Shrimp and Angel Hair Pasta

1 tablespoon vegetable oil
1 tablespoon oriental sesame oil
1 pound large fresh shrimp, peeled, deveined
5 cloves garlic, minced
1 teaspoon minced gingerroot
3/4 cup chicken stock or reduced-sodium broth
1/4 cup dry sherry
2 tablespoons oyster sauce
1 tablespoon cold water
2 teaspoons cornstarch
Salt and pepper to taste
10 ounces angel hair pasta
1/4 cup chopped fresh cilantro

Warm the vegetable oil and sesame oil in a large heavy skillet over medium-high heat. Add the shrimp, garlic and ginger. Sauté for 2 minutes or until the shrimp are pink. Remove the shrimp to a plate, using a slotted spoon.

Pour the stock, sherry and oyster sauce into the same skillet; stir to blend. Bring to a boil, deglazing the skillet. Whisk the water and cornstarch in a small bowl until the cornstarch dissolves. Pour into the skillet. Boil for 2 minutes or until thickened to the consistency of a sauce, stirring constantly. Return the shrimp to the skillet. Season with the salt and pepper. Remove from the heat.

Fill a large pot with salted water, and bring to a boil over high heat. Add the angel hair pasta. Cook until al dente; drain. Add to the shrimp mixture, and toss to coat. Remove to a serving bowl. Sprinkle the cilantro over the pasta.

Yield: 4 servings

Spicy Seafood and Shells

1 (28-ounce) can Italian plum tomatoes
3 tablespoons olive oil
3 large cloves garlic, chopped
1/2 teaspoon dried crushed red pepper flakes
1 (10-ounce) can small clams, drained, liquid reserved
4 tablespoons chopped fresh parsley

1 teaspoon dried basil, crumbled
1 teaspoon anchovy paste (optional)
Salt to taste
12 ounces large shell pasta
12 ounces large shrimp, peeled, deveined
Pepper to taste

Chop the plum tomatoes, reserving the juice. Warm the oil in a large heavy skillet over medium heat. Add the garlic and dried red pepper. Sauté for 1 minute or until fragrant. Stir in the tomatoes with juice, reserved clam liquid, 2 tablespoons of the parsley, the basil and anchovy paste. Cook, covered, for 15 minutes. Uncover. Simmer for 15 minutes or until the mixture thickens, stirring occasionally.

Fill a large pot with salted water, and bring to a boil over high heat. Add the pasta shells. Cook until al dente; drain.

Add the clams and shrimp to the tomato mixture; mix well. Simmer for 3 minutes or just until the shrimp are cooked through. Season with the salt and pepper. Add the shells to the sauce, and toss to combine. Remove to a large bowl. Sprinkle the remaining 2 tablespoons parsley over the shells and seafood.

Yield: 4 servings

Sun-Dried Tomatoes and Feta over Spaghetti

1	cup sun-dried tomatoes, chopped	2	tablespoons extra-virgin olive oil
1	(12-ounce) can evaporated skim milk (1^1/2 cups)	1	pound cooked cleaned shrimp Salt to taste
1^1/2	cups fat-free cottage cheese	1	pound spaghetti
2	cloves garlic, quartered	4	ounces feta cheese, crumbled
^{1}/2	teaspoon salt	^{3}/4	cup packed chopped fresh basil leaves
^{1}/2	teaspoon freshly ground pepper		
^{1}/8	teaspoon red pepper flakes (optional)		

Place the tomatoes in a bowl and pour in hot water to cover. Let stand for 10 minutes. Drain well.

Combine the evaporated milk, cottage cheese, garlic, ^{1}/2 teaspoon salt, pepper and red pepper in a blender jar. Process until smooth. Add the oil in a stream, processing constantly at high speed until well blended. Pour into a heavy saucepan. Stir in the shrimp. Cook over low heat until hot; do not boil.

Fill a large pot with salted water, and bring to a boil over high heat. Add the spaghetti. Cook until al dente; drain. Remove to a large serving bowl. Pour the shrimp mixture over the spaghetti. Add the tomatoes, cheese and basil; toss to combine.

Hint: The sauce may be made ahead and stored, covered, in the refrigerator. Add the shrimp and heat while the pasta is cooking. Crumbled cooked sausage may be substituted for the shrimp.

Yield: 6 servings

Sides On The Sideboard

For storing silverware or hosting buffets, dining room sideboards lend both decoration and function to our homes. The wonderful side dishes described in this section also enhance the appearance of your entrée, while balancing your meal nutritionally. So sidle up to the table and enjoy!

**Designer
Ann Fletcher**

**Photographer
Weldon
Brewster**

131

Grilled Vegetables with Five-Alarm Marinade

A delicious all-purpose marinade for meats and vegetables.

6	cloves garlic, minced	1/4	cup oyster sauce
2	tablespoons minced gingerroot	1/4	cup soy sauce
	Grated peel of 2 limes	1/4	cup honey
	Juice of 2 limes	1	tablespoon Asian chili sauce
1/2	cup chopped fresh mint leaves	8	to 12 cups assorted vegetables (such as
1/2	cup chopped fresh cilantro		asparagus, carrots, sliced eggplant, green
1/2	cup chopped fresh basil leaves		beans, green onions, mushrooms, sliced
3	green onions, minced		onions, sliced bell peppers, sliced
8	serrano chiles, seeded, minced		potatoes, sliced summer squash,
1/2	cup extra-virgin olive oil		tomatoes, corn, artichokes)
1/2	cup dry sherry		

Combine the garlic, gingerroot, lime peel, lime juice, mint, cilantro, basil, green onions, chiles, oil, sherry, oyster sauce, soy sauce, honey and chili sauce in a noncorrosive bowl (stainless, glass). Add vegetables and marinate for 1 to 2 hours, turning occasionally.

Fire up the grill. Brush the grill rack with oil; place it on the grill. Arrange the vegetables on the rack. Grill for 8 to 10 minutes or until the vegetables soften and begin to turn golden, turning every 5 minutes and brushing on the marinade.

Yield: 6 servings

Designer
Cynthia
Bennett

Photographer
Weldon
Brewster

Classic White Sauce

Thin Sauce:

Margarine	*2 tablespoons*
Flour	*2 tablespoons*
Milk	*2 cups*
Salt and pepper to taste	

Medium Sauce:

Margarine	*1/4 cup*
Flour	*1/4 cup*
Milk	*2 cups*
Salt and pepper to taste	

Thick Sauce:

Margarine	*6 tablespoons*
Flour	*6 tablespoons*
Milk	*2 cups*
Salt and pepper to taste	

Directions:

Melt margarine in saucepan over low heat. Stir in flour until smooth. Add milk gradually, stirring constantly. Cook over medium heat until bubbly, stirring constantly. Season with salt and pepper to taste.

Peas with Pancetta

2	tablespoons olive oil
3/4	cup finely chopped onion
3	ounces pancetta, crisp-fried, crumbled
2	(10-ounce) packages frozen tiny peas, thawed
1/4	cup finely chopped fresh Italian parsley
3	tablespoons canned beef broth
	Salt and pepper to taste

Warm 2 tablespoons oil in a large heavy skillet over medium-low heat. Add the onion. Sauté for 5 minutes or until tender. Stir in the pancetta, peas, parsley and broth.

Cook for 3 minutes or until the peas are heated through. Season with the salt and pepper.

Hint: Use bacon if pancetta is unavailable. Pancetta is an Italian bacon cured in salt and found at Italian markets, some specialty foods stores and some supermarkets.

Yield: 6 servings

Crunchy Potato Casserole

1/4 cup plus 2 tablespoons butter
1 (10 3/4-ounce) can cream of chicken soup
2 cups sour cream
1 1/2 cups shredded Cheddar cheese
6 to 8 medium cooked potatoes
1/3 cup chopped green onions
1 to 1 1/2 cups crushed cornflakes

Preheat the oven to 350 degrees.

Combine 1/4 cup of the butter and the soup in a saucepan. Cook until hot. Blend in the sour cream and cheese. Add the potatoes; whip with a hand-held mixer until creamy and fluffy. Stir in the green onions. Spoon into a 2 1/2-quart baking dish.

Melt the remaining 2 tablespoons butter in a small saucepan. Place the cornflakes in a medium bowl. Pour in the melted butter; toss to coat. Sprinkle over the potato mixture. Bake for 45 minutes.

Hint: May be made ahead and stored, covered, in the refrigerator for 1 day. Top with the cornflakes just before baking.

Yield: 10 servings

Classic White Sauce Variations

Cheese Sauce:
Add 1/2 cup sharp Cheddar cheese
2 drops Worcestershire sauce
Use with broccoli, brussels sprouts, cabbage, macaroni, cauliflower

Curry Sauce:
Add 2 to 3 tablespoons curry powder
1/8 teaspoon ginger
Use with asparagus, carrots, mushrooms, squash

Dill Sauce:
Add 1 to 2 teaspoons dillweed
Use with cauliflower, green beans

Creamy Potato Casserole

A terrific side dish for any holiday menu.

4½ to 5 pounds (about 8 large) russet potatoes, peeled, chopped
1 cup sour cream
8 ounces cream cheese, at room temperature

2 teaspoons garlic salt
½ teaspoon pepper
¼ cup (or more) butter or margarine
Paprika

Butter a 3- or 4-quart baking dish.

Fill a large saucepan with 2 inches water, and bring to a boil. Add the potatoes. Cook, covered, for 40 minutes or until tender; drain. Mash well.

Preheat the oven to 400 degrees.

Beat the sour cream and cream cheese in a small mixer bowl at medium speed until smooth. Add the potatoes, a few spoonfuls at a time, beating until smooth and well blended. Beat in the garlic salt and pepper.

Spoon the mixture into the baking dish. Dot with ¼ cup butter; sprinkle the paprika over the top. Bake, covered, for 50 to 60 minutes or until heated through.

Hint: May be made ahead and stored, covered, in the refrigerator for up to 3 days; bring to room temperature before baking.

Yield: 15 servings

Garlic Mashed Potatoes

10	potatoes, peeled, chopped	1	cup butter
6	cloves garlic, coarsely chopped	1¼	cups sour cream
8	ounces cream cheese, softened	2	teaspoons salt
		1	teaspoon pepper

Pour 2 to 3 inches of water into a large saucepan, and bring to a boil. Add the potatoes and garlic. Cook, covered, until tender; drain. Mash until smooth and creamy. Add the cream cheese, butter, sour cream, salt and pepper, and mix well. Spoon into a 3- or 4-quart baking dish.

Preheat the oven to 350 degrees. Bake for 30 minutes.

Hint: May be made a day ahead and baked just before serving.

Yield: 10 servings

Peppers with Almonds

¼	cup virgin olive oil	1½	teaspoons sugar
3	medium red bell peppers, cut into ¼-inch slices	¼	cup toasted slivered or coarsely chopped almonds
2	medium green bell peppers, cut into ¼-inch slices	¼	cup red wine vinegar
½	cup raisins		Salt to taste

Warm the oil in a skillet over medium heat. Add the bell peppers. Sauté until golden and soft but not limp. Stir in the raisins. Cook for 2 minutes. Stir in the sugar. Stir in the almonds. Pour in the vinegar and season with the salt. Cook for 5 minutes. Serve hot or at room temperature.

Hint: May be made ahead and stored, covered, in the refrigerator for up to 3 days.

Yield: 6 servings

Tips For Healthy Living

We can influence our health enormously by following some general guidelines. Control of high blood pressure, obesity, and diabetes, cessation of smoking, and maintaining a favorable cholesterol level are all beneficial to health. We have little control over our family history, though we can control factors that influence a healthy lifestyle.

Eating a healthful diet and getting enough exercise are the best ways to influence your health.

**Designer
Ursula Brown**

**Photographer
Cameron
Carothers**

Dining Tips

1. *Arrive on time at a party—not early, not late.*
2. *Seating can make or break a party. Always have a seating plan (and never switch placecards!).*
3. *The guest of honor is seated to the host's right.*
4. *Begin eating when the hostess lifts her fork.*
5. *Never apply makeup at the table!*
6. *There are two styles of eating: the European (Continental) and the American style. The European is much more chic (and practical!).*
7. *In a restaurant always give your guest the seat with the view.*
8. *Not sure which fork to use? Work from the outside in.*

Designer
John
Fremdling

Photographer
NTA
Associates

Risotto with Portobello Mushrooms

4	tablespoons extra-virgin olive oil
2	tablespoons unsalted butter
8	ounces portobello mushrooms, chopped
$^1/_2$	cup dry white wine
1	small onion, finely chopped
2	cloves garlic, minced
$1^1/_2$	cups arborio rice
6	cups hot beef broth
$^1/_3$	cup grated Parmigiano-Reggiano cheese
	Salt and freshly ground pepper to taste

Warm 1 tablespoon of the oil and 1 tablespoon of the butter in a medium nonstick skillet. Add the mushrooms. Sauté until soft. Stir in $^1/_4$ cup of the wine. Reduce the heat to very low. Cook for 5 minutes. Remove from the heat.

Warm the remaining 3 tablespoons oil in a large heavy saucepan over medium heat. Add the onion. Sauté until soft. Stir in the garlic. Sauté for 1 to 2 minutes or until soft. Stir in the rice. Cook for 3 minutes, stirring constantly. Add the remaining $^1/_4$ cup wine. Cook until the liquid is absorbed, stirring constantly.

Pour in 5 cups of the broth, $^1/_2$ cup at a time, stirring constantly to avoid sticking. Add the next addition of broth as each is absorbed. Stir in the mushrooms.

Pour in the remaining 1 cup broth, stirring as before. Cook until the rice is creamy on the outside and slightly firm in the center, stirring constantly. Add the Parmesan cheese and the remaining 1 tablespoon butter, stirring to mix well. Season with the salt and pepper.

Yield: 4 servings

Stir-Fry Wild Rice

2 cups chicken broth	1/4 cup diced Anaheim chile
1 cup wild rice	1/4 cup bean sprouts
1/4 cup sesame oil	1/4 cup chopped green onions
1/2 cup chopped bok choy	2 tablespoons hoisin sauce
1 tablespoon chopped garlic	2 tablespoons chopped fresh
1 tablespoon chopped gingerroot (optional)	cilantro
1/4 cup julienned red bell pepper	1 teaspoon lime juice

Combine the chicken broth and wild rice in a medium saucepan over medium-low heat. Cook, covered, for 20 minutes or until tender. Remove from the heat; let stand for 10 minutes.

Heat the sesame oil in a wok. Add the bok choy. Stir-fry for 15 seconds. Add the garlic and gingerroot. Stir-fry for 15 seconds. Stir in the bell pepper, Anaheim chile, bean sprouts and green onions. Stir in the wild rice. Stir in the hoisin sauce, cilantro and lime juice. Serve immediately.

Yield: 6 servings

The Foundation

The base of your house upon which everything rests, the foundation is the all-important center of your home. But the kitchen seems to be the center of all social activity, since people always gather there most comfortably. Similarly, the main dishes on the following pages are the centerpiece of your meal, whether you prefer lamb, beef, fish, poultry, or pork. Tonight, build a great foundation.

**Designer
Judy
Campbell**

**Photographer
Phillip Nilsson**

Pork Roast with Thyme and Oregano

4	pounds boneless pork roast	1	medium onion, sliced
2	to 4 tablespoons olive oil	1	cup chicken broth
2	teaspoons salt	1	cup white wine
1	teaspoon pepper	1	clove garlic, minced
1	teaspoon thyme	$1/3$	teaspoon ground nutmeg
1	teaspoon oregano	2	tablespoons butter
4	tablespoons flour	1	cup sour cream

Rub the pork lightly with the oil. Combine the salt, pepper, thyme, oregano and 2 tablespoons of the flour in a small bowl. Rub over the pork, coating it well. Arrange the onion slices on the pork; secure with wooden picks. Chill, covered with waxed paper, in the refrigerator for 10 to 12 hours. Remove to a roasting pan; discard the onion slices.

Preheat the oven to 375 degrees. Roast the pork for 30 minutes. Combine the broth, wine, garlic and nutmeg in a saucepan. Cook until hot.

Reduce the oven temperature to 325 degrees. Pour the broth mixture over the roast. Roast for 1 hour or until a meat thermometer registers 155 degrees, basting often. Remove to a warm platter.

Skim the fat from the basting liquid. Reserve enough of the liquid to measure 2 cups, adding more broth and wine if necessary. Melt the butter in a saucepan; stir in the remaining 2 tablespoons flour. Cook for 2 minutes. Pour in the 2 cups basting liquid and sour cream, whisking until smooth. Cook until thick; do not boil. Carve the roast into $1/2$-inch slices. Serve with the gravy.

Yield: 16 servings

Roast Pork with Apple Topping

Delightful for Sunday dinner.

2	tablespoons flour
1³/4	teaspoons salt
1	teaspoon dry mustard
1	teaspoon caraway seeds
¹/2	teaspoon sugar
¹/4	teaspoon pepper
¹/4	teaspoon dried sage
1	(4-pound) pork loin roast
	Nonstick cooking spray
1¹/2	cups applesauce
¹/2	cup packed dark brown sugar
¹/4	teaspoon allspice

Combine the flour, 1¹/2 teaspoons of the salt, mustard, caraway, sugar, pepper and sage in a small bowl. Rub over the pork. Cover and let stand for 30 minutes. Preheat the oven to 350 degrees. Arrange the roast fat side up on a baking rack coated with the cooking spray in a roasting pan. Roast, uncovered, for 1 hour.

Combine the applesauce, brown sugar, allspice and the remaining ¹/4 teaspoon salt in a small bowl. Spread over the pork. Roast for 1 hour or until a meat thermometer registers 160 to 170 degrees. Let stand for 15 minutes before slicing.

Yield: 8 servings

Caraway

Use the whole seeds in breads, especially rye, and with cheese, sauerkraut and cabbage dishes.

Sage

This herb is a perennial favorite with all kinds of poultry and stuffings.

Orange Ginger Pork Loin Roast

Tasty and low in fat.

3/4	teaspoon dried rosemary		1/4	to 1/2 cup white wine or water
1/2	teaspoon ground ginger		2	tablespoons orange marmalade
1/2	teaspoon dried sage		2	teaspoons Dijon mustard
1/2	teaspoon salt		1/2	cup chicken broth
1/4	teaspoon pepper		1 1/4	teaspoons cornstarch
1	teaspoon sugar		2	teaspoons cold water
2	pounds pork loin roast			

Preheat the oven to 425 degrees.

Combine the rosemary, ginger, sage, salt, pepper and sugar in a small bowl. Rub over the pork. Place in a roasting pan. Roast, uncovered, for 20 minutes.

Pour in the wine; the amount will vary depending on the pan size. Form a tent with foil; place over the pork. Roast for 10 minutes.

Combine 1 tablespoon of the marmalade and 1 teaspoon of the mustard in a measuring cup. Spread over the pork. Roast, uncovered, for 15 minutes or until a meat thermometer registers at least 145 degrees. Remove to a warm platter. Cover with foil to keep warm.

Place the roasting pan over low heat on the stovetop. Stir in the remaining 1 tablespoon marmalade, remaining 1 teaspoon mustard and the chicken broth. Deglaze the pan. Bring to a boil, taking care to avoid burning. Mix the cornstarch and 2 teaspoons cold water in a measuring cup. Pour into the marmalade mixture. Slice the pork into 1/4- to 1/2-inch slices. Spoon the sauce over the pork and serve. Serve with yams and a green vegetable.

Yield: 6 servings

Chili-Spiced Pork Tenderloin

1/4 cup Dijon mustard
1/4 cup honey
1/4 teaspoon salt

1/4 teaspoon chili powder
1   (2-pound) pork tenderloin
     roast

Combine the mustard, honey, salt and chili powder in a small bowl. Spread over the pork. Chill, covered, in the refrigerator for 4 to 24 hours.

Preheat the oven to 425 degrees. Arrange the roast in a foil-lined shallow baking dish. Roast for 1 hour. Let cool for 5 minutes. Slice diagonally.

Hint: Serve with mango chutney. May create a sauce with the mustard, honey salt, chili powder and sour cream. May be made a day ahead and stored, covered, in the refrigerator.

Yield: 4 servings

Grilled Rosemary Honey Pork Chops

1 1/4 cups soy sauce
3/4   cup water
1/4   cup packed brown sugar
1/2   cup honey
       Juice of 1/2 lemon

1   bunch fresh chopped rosemary,
     or 1/2 cup chopped dried
4   thick pork chops
     Nonstick cooking spray

Combine the soy sauce, water, brown sugar, honey, lemon juice and rosemary in a bowl. Pour over the pork. Marinate, covered, in the refrigerator for 4 to 12 hours.

Coat the grill rack with the cooking spray. Fire up the grill. Place on the grill. Arrange the pork chops on the rack. Grill over low heat for 40 minutes or until the pork chops are cooked through.

Yield: 4 servings

Rosemary

This pungent herb is expecially good in poultry and fish dishes and in such accompaniments as stuffings.

Baked Pork Chops with Herb Rub

Make it early so you can entertain later.

1½	cups fresh bread crumbs
1	cup chopped fresh parsley
3	medium cloves garlic, minced
½	cup olive oil
	Juice of ½ lemon
2	tablespoons Dijon mustard
2	teaspoons dried thyme
2	teaspoons crushed dried rosemary
	Salt and pepper to taste
8	(1½-inch-thick) pork chops

Preheat the broiler. Combine the bread crumbs, parsley, garlic, oil, lemon juice, mustard, thyme and rosemary in a medium bowl. Season with the salt and pepper. Rub the mixture over both sides of the pork.

Arrange on a broiler pan. Broil for 5 minutes per side or until the pork chops are golden brown, turning once.

Yield: 4 to 6 servings

Sautéed Pork Tenderloins

All the flavor you could want.

1¹/₂ pounds boneless pork tenderloins	2 tablespoons butter or margarine
¹/₄ cup Major Grey chutney, coarse pieces chopped	¹/₂ cup dry white wine
	³/₄ cup whipping cream

Place the pork in a 7x11-inch baking dish. Brush with 2 to 3 tablespoons of the chutney, coating all sides. Chill, covered, in the refrigerator for 30 minutes to 24 hours.

Melt the butter in a large skillet over medium-high heat. Add the pork. Sauté on all sides. Pour in the wine. Reduce the heat. Simmer, covered, for 20 minutes or until the pork is tender. Remove to a warm platter, and cover with foil to keep warm.

Add the remaining 1 to 2 tablespoons chutney to the skillet. Pour in the cream. Bring to a boil over high heat. Cook for 5 minutes or until large bubbles form and the liquid is reduced to about ¹/₂ cup, stirring constantly. Slice the pork across the grain. Top with the chutney sauce.

Yield: 4 servings

Prime Rib

For that special occasion.

1	prime rib of beef		Onion salt
	Curry powder		Pepper

Preheat the oven to 325 degrees. Place the beef, rib side down, in a shallow roasting pan. Rub on the curry powder, onion salt and pepper, creating a thick paste. Use generous amounts of the spices.

Roast for 30 minutes per pound.

Yield: 6 to 10 servings

Steak with Rich French Cream Sauce

Rich, yet so simple.

2	(approximately 1/2 to 3/4 pound each) T-bone or rib eye steaks	5	tablespoons sour cream
		1	teaspoon onion powder
	Salt and pepper to taste	1	teaspoon garlic powder
1/4	cup butter		

Season the steaks with the salt and pepper. Warm a large skillet over medium heat. Arrange the steaks in the skillet. Cook until the steaks reach the desired doneness. Remove to a platter.

Deglaze the skillet with the butter. Stir in the sour cream, onion powder and garlic powder. Cook until the sauce coats the back of a spoon. Serve over the steaks.

Yield: 2 servings

**Designer
Kathleen
Formanack**

**Photographer
Cameron
Carothers**

Roasted Lamb with Herbed Tomato Chutney

A delightfully spicy dish.

Tomato Chutney
1¹/₂ pounds plum tomatoes, peeled, seeded, diced
1¹/₂ cups chopped onion
¹/₃ cup sugar
¹/₃ cup white wine vinegar
1 (1-inch) piece peeled gingerroot, minced
1 pickled jalapeño, seeded, finely chopped

1 teaspoon each coriander seeds and mustard seeds
³/₄ teaspoon salt
1 tablespoon chopped fresh rosemary, or ¹/₄ cup chopped fresh mint leaves

Lamb Roast
1 teaspoon vegetable oil
2¹/₂ pounds lamb roast
 Salt and pepper to taste

For the chutney, toss the tomatoes, onion and sugar gently in a heavy saucepan. Let stand for 2 hours.

Stir in the vinegar, gingerroot, jalapeño, coriander, mustard seeds and salt. Simmer for 10 minutes. Remove the solids to a bowl, using a slotted spoon, and pour the liquid back into the pan. Boil until the liquid is reduced to ¹/₂ cup. Stir in the rosemary and pour over the chutney, stirring gently. Chill, covered, for 2 hours.

For the lamb, preheat the oven to 450 degrees. Warm the oil in a heavy skillet over medium-high heat. Add the roast. Cook for 3 to 4 minutes on each side or until evenly browned. Season with the salt and pepper. Remove to a roasting pan. Roast on the middle oven rack for 15 to 20 minutes or until a meat thermometer registers at least 130 degrees. Remove to a cutting board. Let stand, uncovered, for 10 minutes. Slice and serve with the chutney.

Hint: The chutney may be made 5 days ahead and stored, covered, in the refrigerator. Use gloves when handling the jalapeño.

Yield: 6 to 8 servings

**Designer
Edward
Turrentine**

How to Set a Table

Knowing how to set a table is actually quite easy once you learn the basics. It is amazing to see how many fine restaurants and clubs set a table improperly. Here are some hints to make you look like the "hostess with the mostess" and give you confidence when entertaining.

Utensils:
• Place according to the order of use: start from the outside and work your way in.
• At a formal setting, a dessert spoon and fork are placed above the dinner plate.

Glasses:
• Place according to use with the first course wine glass set to the far right.

(continued on page 177)

Herb Baked Lamb Chops

Great for entertaining.

4	(2-inch thick) lamb chops
	Flour for coating
4	tablespoons butter
$1/2$	cup red wine vinegar
2	tablespoons extra-virgin olive oil
$1/4$	cup lemon juice
3	tablespoons Worcestershire sauce
$1/2$	cup water
$1/2$	teaspoon dried oregano
$1/2$	teaspoon dried thyme
2	bay leaves
$1/4$	teaspoon garlic salt
$1/4$	teaspoon white pepper
2	medium onions, sliced

Preheat the oven to 325 degrees. Coat the lamb with the flour. Melt 2 tablespoons butter in a skillet. Add the lamb. Brown.

Melt the remaining 2 tablespoons butter in a small saucepan. Stir in the vinegar, oil, lemon juice, Worcestershire sauce, water, oregano, thyme, bay leaves, garlic salt and pepper.

Place the chops in a 9x13 baking dish. Pour in the vinegar mixture. Top with the onions. Bake, uncovered, for 2 hours or until a meat thermometer registers at least 145 degrees. Discard the bay leaves before serving.

Yield: 4 servings

Hot Lamb Satay with Mint and Garlic

6   (8-inch) bamboo skewers
1   pound boned leg of lamb, trimmed
1/2   cup hoisin sauce
1/4   cup plum sauce
2   teaspoons grated or finely minced orange peel
1/4   cup dry sherry
2   tablespoons honey
1   tablespoon Asian chili sauce
1/3   cup chopped fresh mint
8   cloves garlic, minced

Soak the bamboo skewers in enough hot water to cover for 1 to 24 hours.

Cut the lamb into sixteen 1/4 x 4-inch strips.

Combine the hoisin sauce, plum sauce, orange peel, sherry, honey, chili sauce, mint and garlic in a small bowl. Thread the lamb onto the skewers and arrange in a shallow baking dish. Pour in the hoisin mixture. Marinate, covered, in the refrigerator for 15 minutes to 2 hours.

Fire up the grill. Brush oil over the grill rack or coat it with the cooking spray. Place on the grill. Arrange the lamb on the rack. Grill for 2 minutes on a side or until the meat is still slightly pink in the center. Remove to a serving plate.

Hint: May also cook under the broiler. Preheat the oven to 550 degrees. Place the broiling rack at the highest position. Arrange the lamb on a baking sheet. Cover the skewer ends with foil. Broil for 2 to 4 minutes on a side or until the meat is still slightly pink in the center.

Yield: 4 servings

How to Set a Table

Plates:

• *The plate on the table where you are seated is the service plate or place plate.*

• *Any food other than that on your dinner plate should be on the left side of your place setting (the bread and butter plate is always on the left).*

Napkins:

• *Pick up the napkin when you sit down at the table. It lays on your lap; not in your belt or tucked under your chin.*

• *When you leave the table temporarily, place your napkin on the chair.*

Stewed Lamb Shanks with White Beans and Rosemary

1	pound dried Great Northern white beans	3	ribs celery, diced
8	(about 1 pound each) lamb shanks, exposed bone removed	1	cup dry red wine
		1	(28-ounce) can whole plum tomatoes packed in tomato purée
4	teaspoons salt		
	Freshly ground pepper to taste	8	cups chicken broth
2	teaspoons olive oil	5	sprigs fresh rosemary
8	large cloves garlic, minced	2	bay leaves
1	large onion, diced		Diced bacon (optional)
4	medium carrots, diced		Salt to taste

Rinse and sort the beans. Soak in water to cover in a stockpot for 8 to 10 hours; drain.

Season the lamb with 1 teaspoon of the salt and the pepper. Warm the oil in a large heavy skillet over medium-high heat. Add as many lamb shanks as will fit without crowding. Brown for 10 minutes on each side or until well browned. Remove to a warm platter. Brown the remaining shanks, draining the skillet between batches.

Add the garlic, onion, carrots and celery to the skillet. Sauté for 10 minutes or until softened. Pour in the wine. Cook for 2 minutes, deglazing with a wooden spoon.

Remove the vegetables and wine to a large stockpot. Add the tomatoes, and use the back of a spoon to break them into bite-size chunks. Add the beans, broth, rosemary, bay leaves, bacon and lamb shanks. Bring to a boil. Reduce the heat. Simmer for 2 hours or until the lamb and beans are very tender, skimming as necessary. Remove the lamb to a warm platter if done before the beans. Cover with foil to keep warm.

Skim the fat from the top of the cooking liquid. Return the shanks to the stockpot. Simmer over low heat until hot. Remove the shanks, using tongs and placing 1 shank on each of 8 plates. Season the bean mixture with additional salt if needed. Arrange the beans and vegetables around each shank, using a slotted spoon. Spoon the liquid over and around the shanks.

Hint: Bacon may be added to the oil for browning. May be made ahead and stored, covered, in the refrigerator for a day. Remove from the refrigerator for 30 minutes before heating.

Yield: 8 servings

Roasted Chicken with Fresh Herbs

2	tablespoons minced fresh basil	3	cloves garlic, crushed
1	tablespoon minced fresh oregano	1	(3-pound) chicken
			Nonstick cooking spray
2	teaspoons minced fresh thyme		Sprigs of basil (optional)
1	teaspoon olive oil		Sprigs of oregano (optional)
1/2	teaspoon salt		Sprigs of thyme (optional)
1/2	teaspoon coarsely ground pepper		

Preheat the oven to 375 degrees. Combine the minced basil, minced oregano, minced thyme, oil, salt, pepper and garlic in a small bowl; mix well.

Discard the chicken giblets and neck. Trim excess fat. Loosen the breast skin, starting at the neck, by gently sliding fingers between the meat and skin. Insert the herb mixture under the skin. Tie the legs together. Lift the wing tips and tuck under the chicken. Insert a meat thermometer into the thickest part of the thigh, not touching the bone. Coat a broiler pan with the cooking spray.

Roast for 1 hour or until the thermometer registers 180 degrees. Cover loosely with foil; let stand for 10 minutes. Discard the skin. Garnish with the herb sprigs.

Yield: 4 servings

Tangy Orange Chicken

A weekday staple.

8	boneless, skinless chicken breasts	2	bay leaves
1	(12-ounce) can frozen orange juice concentrate, thawed		Pinch of garlic salt
1	(12-ounce) bottle chili sauce	6	tablespoons tomato paste
			Orange slices (optional)

Preheat the oven to 350 degrees. Arrange the chicken in a large baking dish.

Combine the orange juice concentrate, chili sauce, bay leaves, garlic salt and tomato paste in a bowl and mix well. Pour over the chicken. Bake, covered, for 20 minutes. Turn the chicken. Bake for 25 minutes. Serve with rice and the orange slices.

Yield: 8 servings

Ginger Chicken

Great family fare.

1/4	cup soy sauce	1	cup packed dark brown sugar
1	cup water	1	whole chicken, cut into pieces,
2	tablespoons grated gingerroot		skin removed, or 4 boneless,
3	tablespoons butter		skinless breasts

Pour the soy sauce and water into a large skillet. Stir in the gingerroot, butter and brown sugar. Bring the mixture to a simmer.

Add the chicken to the soy sauce mixture. Simmer for 45 minutes or until cooked through, turning and basting occasionally. Serve over steamed rice.

Yield: 4 servings

Chicken with Parmesan Cream

This chicken is so tender, you can slice it with a fork.

4	boneless, skinless chicken breasts, filleted
1/2	cup flour
6	tablespoons butter
16	sliced mushrooms
1	cup whipping cream
	Salt and pepper to taste
2/3	cup grated Parmesan cheese
	Paprika to taste

Coat the chicken with the flour. Melt 3 tablespoons of the butter in a small saucepan over low heat or in a small microwave-safe bowl in the microwave. Dip the chicken in the butter. Arrange in a 9x13-inch baking dish.

Melt the remaining 3 tablespoons butter in a medium skillet. Add the mushrooms. Sauté. Spread over the chicken. Pour in the cream. Season with the salt and pepper, and top with the Parmesan cheese. Chill, covered with plastic wrap, in the refrigerator for 12 hours.

Preheat the oven to 400 degrees. Sprinkle the paprika over the mixture. Bake, uncovered, for 20 to 30 minutes or until the chicken is cooked through and the juices are clear. Serve with a green vegetable.

Yield: 6 to 8 servings

Paprika

A mild pepper that adds color to many dishes, the very best paprika is imported from Hungary.

A Gracious Gift

A homemade meal can be a welcome and comforting gift for new mothers, families in mourning, or a neighbor who just moved in next door. Here are a few hints in preparing a gift of this type:

- *Be sure to use disposable baking pans so the recipient does not need to return your dish.*
- *Paper plates and plastic flatware are also helpful.*
- *As with any meal, presentation is important. Fresh flowers, candles for the dinner table, and colorful tissue lining the box or bag for transporting the meal add a special touch.*

**Designer
Cynthia
Bennett**

**Photographer
Alexander
Vertikoff**

**Pasadena Showcase
House of Design**

Spanish Paella

Authentic Spanish paella—it's the real thing!

1	boneless, skinless chicken breast
1	pork chop (optional)
4	cups chicken broth
1/4	cup olive oil
1/2	red bell pepper, diced
1	tomato, seeded, diced
3	cloves garlic, minced
1	cup sliced mushrooms
2	cups arborio rice
12	large shrimp, peeled, deveined
1/4	teaspoon saffron
6	clams
6	mussels

Place the chicken and pork in a microwave-safe dish. Pour in 1/2 cup of the broth. Cover with waxed paper. Microwave for 10 minutes or until cooked through. Chop the chicken and pork, reserving the liquid.

Warm the oil in a large skillet until hot but not sizzling. Add the vegetables. Sauté for 5 minutes. Stir in the rice. Sauté for 2 minutes. Stir in the pork, chicken and shrimp. Sauté for 1 minute.

Stir in the remaining broth, the reserved cooking liquid and the saffron. Bring to a boil. Stir in the clams and mussels. Reduce the heat. Simmer, covered, for 20 minutes or until the clams and mussels open, the shrimp turn pink and the rice is tender and the liquid evaporated, adding more water if necessary.

Yield: 6 servings

Fragrant Food

When running late in preparing dinner, start the preparation by sautéing onions, which will create the impression that a culinary masterpiece is in progress.

You can also create that home-cooked smell by lighting food-scented candles: sugar cookie, apple pie, and pumpkin spice all create the idea that baking has just occurred. If you don't have candles on hand, try simmering cinnamon sticks and cloves in apple juice on your stove, or brew a pot of coffee.

**Designer
Ria Zake Jacob**

**Photographer
Cameron
Carothers**

Caribbean Swordfish with Thai Banana Salsa

Not a single bite will be left.

Thai Banana Salsa
2 medium firm slightly green bananas, chopped
1 red bell pepper, chopped
1/4 cup chopped fresh cilantro
2 tablespoons minced gingerroot
2 tablespoons freshly squeezed orange juice
2 tablespoons freshly squeezed lime juice
2 tablespoons brown sugar

2 tablespoons fish sauce
2 teaspoons Thai chili sauce

Caribbean Swordfish
1 1/2 pounds swordfish
3 tablespoons light soy sauce
3 tablespoons dry sherry or rice wine
2 tablespoons oyster sauce
2 tablespoons vegetable oil
1 tablespoon honey

For the salsa, combine the bananas, bell pepper, cilantro, gingerroot, orange juice, lime juice, brown sugar, fish sauce and Thai chili sauce in a small bowl within 2 hours of serving.

For the swordfish, combine the swordfish, soy sauce, sherry, oyster sauce, oil and honey in a large shallow bowl. Marinate for at least 15 minutes but not longer than 4 hours.

Fire up the grill. Brush the grill rack with oil. Arrange the swordfish on the rack. Grill for 8 minutes or until the fish is done and feels firm to the touch. Serve at once with the banana salsa.

Yield: 4 servings

Lemon Thyme Swordfish

6	(6-ounce) swordfish steaks, ½ inch thick, skin removed	2	tablespoons coarse mustard
	Juice of 2 lemons	¼	cup olive oil
2	shallots, thinly sliced	3	or 4 sprigs of fresh thyme, minced
2	cloves garlic, crushed		Freshly ground pepper

Place the swordfish in a shallow bowl. Whisk the lemon juice, shallots, garlic, mustard, oil and thyme in a small bowl. Season with the pepper. Pour over the swordfish. Marinate, covered, at room temperature for 30 minutes, or in the refrigerator for several hours.

Fire up the grill. Brush the grill rack with oil. Arrange the swordfish on the rack. Grill for 3 to 4 minutes per side or until seared on the outside and cooked through.

Yield: 6 servings

a memory

My husband stumbled upon a chile shrimp recipe in a magazine. It was similar to a dish we had eaten at a restaurant when we were dating. With a few of our own additions, the dish tasted just as we fondly remembered.

Chile Shrimp Stir-Fry

1	tablespoon canola or peanut oil
1	pound large shrimp, peeled, deveined
1	tablespoon minced gingerroot
3	cloves garlic, minced
1/4	to 1/2 cup cashews
3	tablespoons ketchup
1	tablespoon cider vinegar
1	tablespoon soy sauce
1	tablespoon sugar
1/2	to 1 teaspoon crushed red chiles
1/2	teaspoon sesame oil
3	cups rice, cooked, kept warm
	Sliced green onions

Warm the canola oil in a wok or large skillet over high heat. Add the shrimp. Stir-fry for 3 minutes or until pink and opaque. Remove the shrimp, using a slotted spoon.

Place the gingerroot, garlic and cashews in the same wok. Stir-fry for 30 seconds or until the garlic is tinged with gold. Stir in the ketchup, vinegar, soy sauce, sugar and chiles. Bring to a boil, stirring constantly.

Add the shrimp and sesame oil. Toss to combine. Mound the rice on a platter; top with the shrimp mixture and green onions.

Yield: 4 servings

Thai Shrimp and Noodles

8 ounces spaghetti, broken
1½ pounds (about 5 cups) broccoli florets
1 pound shrimp, peeled, deveined
⅓ cup creamy peanut butter
¼ to ⅓ cup soy sauce
2 tablespoons rice vinegar
2 tablespoons sesame oil

1 tablespoon chili oil, or
1 tablespoon vegetable oil plus a dash of hot pepper sauce
1 tablespoon grated gingerroot
3 cloves garlic, minced
4 green onions, chopped
⅓ cup chopped cashews or almonds

Fill a large saucepan with water, and bring to a boil. Add the spaghetti. Cook for 4 minutes. Add the broccoli. Cook for 2 minutes. Add the shrimp. Cook for 2 to 3 minutes or until the shrimp is pink.

Combine the peanut butter and soy sauce in a bowl. Stir in the vinegar, sesame and chili oils, the gingerroot and garlic. Drain the pasta mixture. Add the peanut butter mixture, green onions and cashews; toss to coat.

Yield: 6 servings

Decorative Decadence

When it is time to treat yourself, a warm bath can provide the perfect respite. A fabulous dessert can accomplish the same thing. Choose from our extensive array of both easy and gourmet recipes. Soon, you will fully understand the phrase, "Home, Sweet Home."

**Designer
John
Fremdling**

**Photographer
Martin Fine**

Italian Cream Cake

Coconut Cake
	Flour for dusting
1/2	cup unsalted butter, softened
1/2	cup shortening
2	cups sugar
5	egg yolks
2	cups flour
1	teaspoon baking soda
1	cup buttermilk
1	teaspoon vanilla extract
1	(8-ounce) package flaked coconut
1	cup walnuts, finely chopped
5	egg whites, stiffly beaten

Vanilla Frosting
8	ounces cream cheese, softened
1/4	cup unsalted butter, softened
2	cups confectioners' sugar
1	teaspoon vanilla extract
	Flaked coconut (optional)

For the cake, preheat the oven to 350 degrees. Grease three 9-inch-round cake pans. Dust with the flour. Beat the butter and shortening in a large bowl. Add the sugar, beating until smooth. Add the egg yolks, beating well. Combine the 2 cups flour and baking soda in a medium bowl. Mix into the creamed mixture, alternating with the buttermilk and beginning and ending with the buttermilk. Stir in the vanilla. Mix in the coconut and walnuts; fold in the egg whites. Pour into the pans. Bake for 25 minutes. Let cool on wire racks. Remove from the pans, and finish cooling on racks.

For the frosting, beat the cream cheese and butter in a medium bowl until smooth. Mix in the confectioners' sugar and vanilla, beating until smooth. Frost the cake.

Decorate with the flaked coconut.

Yield: 10 servings

a memory

This was our wedding cake. Instead of using a local bakery, we flew a woman from Washington, D.C., in to make our cake. My husband had tasted her cake while interning for congress when he was in college.

Designer
Tracy Larsen

Photographer
Rachel
Olguin

Pasadena Showcase
House of Design

Zesty Lemon Mousse

6	egg yolks		1	cup whipping cream
3/4	cup sugar		6	egg whites
	Grated peel of 1 lemon			Thin lemon slices
	Juice of 3 large lemons			

Beat the egg yolks, 1/2 cup of the sugar and lemon peel in the top of a double boiler until pale yellow. Place over boiling water. Stir in the lemon juice. Cook for 3 to 5 minutes or until the mixture has doubled in volume, beating constantly with a wire whisk. Place the top of the double boiler in a large bowl of ice water. Whisk until cool.

Beat the cream in a large bowl until medium thick.

Beat the egg whites and remaining 1/4 cup sugar in another large bowl until stiff peaks form. Fold the cream into the lemon mixture; fold in the egg whites, blending thoroughly. Spoon into individual dessert glasses.

Chill, covered with plastic wrap, in the refrigerator. Decorate each serving with the lemon slices.

Yield: 6 to 8 servings

**Designer
Robin
Dorman**

**Photographer
Weldon
Brewster**

Chocolate Silk Cake with a Nut Crust

Tastes like a silk ribbon of mouthwatering chocolate.

Nut Crust

3/4 cup walnuts, toasted, coarsely chopped
1   cup pecans, toasted, coarsely chopped
1/2 cup packed brown sugar
     Pinch of cinnamon
1/2 cup unsalted butter, melted

Chocolate Mousse

20   ounces bittersweet chocolate
3/4 cup unsalted butter, softened
3/4 cup sugar
6   eggs
1/4 cup whipping cream
1/2 teaspoon vanilla extract

Cream Topping

1/2 cup whipping cream
2   tablespoons sugar

For the crust, combine the walnuts, pecans, brown sugar and cinnamon in a bowl; stir in the butter. Press over the bottom of a 9-inch springform pan. Chill, covered, in the refrigerator or freezer while making the mousse.

For the mousse, melt the chocolate in the top of a double boiler over simmering water. Cool. Cream the butter and sugar in the mixer bowl of an electric mixer at medium-high speed. Stir in the eggs, two at a time; the mixture will look curdled. Whisk the chocolate into the egg mixture at medium speed. Whisk for 2 minutes, scraping the bottom and side of the bowl frequently. Stir in the cream and vanilla. Pour into the crust. Chill, covered, in the refrigerator for 12 hours.

For the topping, whip the cream and sugar until soft peaks form. Spread over the mousse.

Yield: 10 servings

Cuban Cheesecake Flan

A unique cross between a cheesecake and a flan.

1/2	cup sugar	8	ounces cream cheese, softened and cubed
1	(12-ounce) can evaporated milk	3	eggs
1	(14-ounce) can sweetened condensed milk	1	teaspoon vanilla extract

Warm the sugar in a saucepan over low heat for 8 to 10 minutes or until melted and straw colored, stirring constantly. Spread evenly in the bottom of a 9-inch deep-dish pie plate; let cool. Combine the evaporated milk, condensed milk, cream cheese, eggs and vanilla in a blender jar. Process until smooth. Pour into the pie plate.

Place the pie plate in a large pan; pour water into the pan to 1/2 to 3/4 inch deep. Bake at 350 degrees for 55 to 60 minutes or until set. Let cool. Chill, covered, in the refrigerator.

Run a knife around the edge of the cheesecake; invert onto a serving plate. Cut into wedges.

Yield: 10 to 12 servings

Pumpkin Cheesecake with Bourbon Sour Cream Topping

A beautiful presentation for your holiday table.

Crumb Crust

3/4 cup graham cracker crumbs
1/2 cup finely chopped pecans
1/4 cup packed light brown sugar
1/4 cup sugar
1/4 cup butter, melted, cooled

Pumpkin Filling

1 (15-ounce) can solid-pack pumpkin
3 eggs
2 teaspoons ground cinnamon
3/4 teaspoon ground nutmeg
1/2 teaspoon ground ginger
1/2 teaspoon salt
1/2 cup packed light brown sugar
24 ounces cream cheese, softened
1/2 cup sugar
2 tablespoons whipping cream
1 tablespoon cornstarch
1 teaspoon vanilla extract
1 tablespoon bourbon

Bourbon Sour Cream Topping

2 cups sour cream
2 tablespoons sugar
1 tablespoon bourbon
16 pecan halves

For the crust, butter a 9-inch springform pan. Combine the crumbs, pecans, brown sugar and sugar in a bowl. Stir in the melted butter. Press the mixture over the bottom and 1/2 inch up the side of the pan. Chill, covered, in the refrigerator for 1 hour.

For the filling, preheat the oven to 350 degrees. Whisk the pumpkin, eggs, cinnamon, nutmeg, ginger, salt and brown sugar in a large bowl. Cut the cream cheese into chunks and cream together with the sugar in the large bowl of an electric mixer. Beat in the cream, cornstarch, vanilla, bourbon and the pumpkin mixture until smooth.

Pour into the crust. Bake on the middle rack of the oven for 50 to 55 minutes or until the center is set. Let cool in the pan on a wire rack for 5 minutes.

For the topping, whisk the sour cream, sugar and bourbon in a bowl. Spread over the cheesecake. Bake for 5 minutes. Let cool in the pan on a wire rack. Chill, covered, for 12 hours. Remove the side; decorate with the pecans.

Yield: 10 to 12 servings

Chocolate Cheesecake

Cracker Crumb Crust
Nonstick cooking spray
1/4 cup butter or margarine, melted
1 cup graham cracker crumbs
1/4 cup sweet ground chocolate
1/4 cup sugar
1/8 teaspoon cinnamon

Cream Cheese Filling
24 ounces cream cheese, softened
3/4 cup sugar
1/2 cup sweet ground chocolate
1 tablespoon vanilla extract
4 eggs

Chocolate Topping
1 cup sour cream
2 tablespoons sweet ground chocolate
1/4 cup sugar

For the crust, preheat the oven to 350 degrees. Coat an 8-inch springform pan with the cooking spray.

Combine the butter, crumbs, chocolate, sugar and cinnamon in a food processor bowl. Process to mix. Press over the bottom of the prepared pan. Bake for 6 minutes. Let cool.

For the filling, beat the cream cheese in a large bowl until smooth, gradually adding the sugar, chocolate and vanilla. Add the eggs, one at a time, mixing until smooth after each addition. Pour into the crust. Bake for 40 to 45 minutes or until a knife inserted in the center comes out clean. Cool completely.

For the topping, whisk the sour cream, chocolate and sugar in a small bowl. Spread over the cheesecake. Bake at 350 degrees for 5 minutes. Chill, covered, for several hours.

Yield: 12 servings

Red Velvet Cake

Perfect for Valentine's Day.

Red Velvet Cake
- Nonstick cooking spray
- Flour for dusting
- 1/2 cup shortening
- 1 1/2 cups sugar
- 2 eggs
- 2 tablespoons baking cocoa
- 2 ounces red food coloring
- 2 1/4 cups flour
- 1 teaspoon salt
- 1 cup buttermilk
- 1 teaspoon vanilla extract
- 1 tablespoon vinegar
- 1 teaspoon baking soda

Butter Frosting
- 1 cup milk
- 3 tablespoons flour
- 1 cup sugar
- 1 cup butter, softened
- 1 teaspoon vanilla extract

For the cake, preheat the oven to 350 degrees. Coat two 9-inch-round cake pans with the cooking spray. Dust with the flour.

Cream the shortening, sugar and eggs in a large bowl. Combine the cocoa and food coloring to make a paste. Blend into the shortening mixture. Add, in the order listed, the 2 1/4 cups flour, the salt, buttermilk and vanilla, mixing well. Combine the vinegar and baking soda. Fold into the batter.

Pour into the pans. Bake for 25 to 30 minutes. Let cool on wire racks.

For the frosting, combine the milk and flour in a saucepan. Cook over low heat until the mixture is thick and coats the back of a spoon. Remove from the heat; let cool.

Cream the sugar, butter and vanilla in a bowl. Add the milk mixture, beating with an electric mixer for 8 to 10 minutes or until creamy. Spread over the cake layers.

Yield: 10 to 12 servings

**Designer
Kathleen
Formanack**

**Photographer
Cameron
Carothers**

Fourteen-Carat Cake with Penuche Frosting

Pineapple Carrot Cake
Nonstick cooking spray
Flour for dusting
1 (8³/₈-ounce) can crushed pineapple
2 cups flour
1¹/₂ teaspoons baking soda
2 teaspoons baking powder
1 teaspoon salt
2 teaspoons cinnamon
2 cups sugar

1 cup vegetable oil
4 eggs
2 cups shredded carrots
¹/₂ cup chopped walnuts (optional)

Penuche Frosting
¹/₂ cup butter
1 cup packed brown sugar
¹/₄ cup warm milk
1³/₄ cups confectioners' sugar

For the cake, preheat the oven to 350 degrees. Coat two 9-inch-round cake pans with the cooking spray. Dust with the flour.

Drain the pineapple, reserving ¹/₂ cup of the juice and adding water if needed to measure ¹/₂ cup. Combine the 2 cups flour, baking soda, baking powder, salt, cinnamon, sugar, oil, eggs and ¹/₂ cup reserved pineapple juice in the mixer bowl of an electric mixer. Beat at medium speed. Stir in the carrots, pineapple and walnuts. Pour into the pans. Bake for 35 to 40 minutes or until a wooden pick inserted in the center comes out clean. Cool completely on wire racks.

For the frosting, melt the butter with the brown sugar in a saucepan. Boil over low heat for 2 minutes, stirring constantly. Stir in the warm milk. Bring to a boil. Remove from the heat. Let cool to lukewarm. Beat in the confectioners' sugar, a little at a time and using an electric mixer, until smooth. Frost the cake.

Yield: 8 to 10 servings

Drunken Chocolate Pecan Cake

Chocolate Pecan Cake
12   ounces semisweet chocolate
1   cup unsalted butter
8   egg yolks
1/2 cup bourbon
1 1/2 cups sugar
8   egg whites
1 1/2 cups whole shelled pecans, ground

Chocolate Frosting
1   pound semisweet chocolate
3/4 cup butter
1/2 cup shelled pecan halves
    Whipped cream

For the cake, preheat the oven to 300 degrees. Melt the chocolate and butter in a saucepan, stirring to blend.

Combine the egg yolks, bourbon and 3/4 cup of the sugar in the top of a double boiler. Cook over simmering water until creamy and light yellow, beating constantly with a wooden spoon.

Beat the egg whites and the remaining 3/4 cup sugar in a large bowl until stiff peaks form. Fold in the egg yolk mixture. Fold in the melted chocolate and the pecans. Spoon into a 10-inch springform pan. Bake for 1 3/4 hours. Let cool in the pan. Remove the pan side.

For the frosting, melt the chocolate and butter in the top of a double boiler over simmering water, stirring constantly until smooth. Let stand until thick enough to spread, stirring frequently. Level the cake top, using a serrated knife. Frost the cooled cake. Decorate with pecan halves. Serve topped with whipped cream.

Yield: 10 to 12 servings

I discovered this cake while watching a PBS cooking show. It was this cake that made my family think I could bake.

Candy Chart

For fudge, penuche and fondant:

Soft ball   *can be picked*
234°-240°   *up but flattens*

For caramels:

Firm ball   *holds shape*
242°-248°   *unless pressed*

For divinity, taffy and caramel corn:

Hard ball   *holds shape*
250°-268°   *though pliable*

Butterscotch and English toffee:

Soft crack   *separates into*
270°-290°   *hard threads*
           but not brittle

Drop about ¹/₂ teaspoon of boiling syrup into 1 cup cold water, and test firmness of mass with fingers.

**Designer
Kathleen
Formanack**

**Photographer
Cameron
Carothers**

Pecan Tartlets

Cream Cheese Pastry

1 cup flour
1/2 cup unsalted butter, slightly softened
3 ounces cream cheese, softened
1/4 teaspoon salt

Pecan Filling

1 egg, slightly beaten
1/2 cup dark corn syrup
1/3 cup packed dark brown sugar
2 tablespoons unsalted butter, melted
1 teaspoon vanilla extract
Pinch of salt
1 cup coarsely broken pecans

Chocolate Topping

2 (1-ounce) squares semisweet chocolate
2 teaspoons vegetable oil

For the pastry, preheat the oven to 350 degrees. Combine the flour, butter, cream cheese and salt in a large bowl; mix until well blended and the dough forms a ball. Divide into 24 equal pieces. Shape each into a ball. Press into small brioche pans or miniature muffin cups. Chill the dough briefly, covered, if it becomes too soft. Press the dough to the sides of the pans, using floured fingers. Cover completely, or the filling will stick.

For the filling, combine the egg, corn syrup, brown sugar, butter, vanilla and salt in a medium bowl, stirring until well blended. Stir in the pecans. Spoon into the pastry. The filling should come almost to the top of the pans but not touch exposed areas of the pans. Bake for 25 to 30 minutes or until the filling is set but the center is still slightly soft. Cool in the pans on wire racks. Loosen the sides, using the tip of a knife. Unmold.

For the topping, melt the chocolate and oil in the top of a double boiler over hot, not simmering, water, stirring constantly. Drizzle over the tartlets, using a spoon or parchment-paper cone. Store in an airtight container at room temperature.

Yield: 24 tartlets

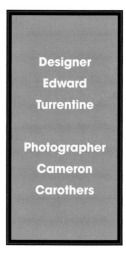

Designer
Edward
Turrentine

Photographer
Cameron
Carothers

Four-Minute Brownie Pie à la Mode

	Nonstick cooking spray
2	eggs
1	cup sugar
1/2	cup butter, softened
1/2	cup flour
4	tablespoons baking cocoa
1	teaspoon vanilla extract
	Pinch of salt
1/2	cup chopped walnuts

Preheat the oven to 325 degrees. Coat a pie pan with the cooking spray. Beat the eggs, sugar, butter, flour, cocoa, vanilla and salt in the small mixing bowl of an electric mixer at high speed for 4 minutes. Stir in the walnuts; pour into the pie pan.

Bake for 30 minutes. The pie will settle when cooled. Slice and serve with vanilla ice cream and Hot Fudge Sauce.

Yield: 6 servings

Hot Fudge Sauce

2	tablespoons butter
2	(1-ounce) squares unsweetened chocolate
1	cup sugar
	Dash of salt
2/3	cup evaporated milk
1	teaspoon vanilla extract

Melt the butter and chocolate in the top of a double boiler over simmering water. Stir in the sugar and salt. Stir the evaporated milk in slowly. Cook for 20 minutes or until thickened. Remove from the heat. Add the vanilla and mix well.

Yield: 4 to 6 servings

Decadent Brownies

½ cup butter
2 (1-ounce) squares unsweetened baking chocolate
½ cup flour
1 cup sugar
1 teaspoon baking powder
1 teaspoon vanilla extract
2 eggs
½ cup chopped walnuts (optional)
   Nonstick cooking spray

Preheat the oven to 350 degrees. Melt the butter and chocolate in a small saucepan. Combine the flour, sugar and baking powder in a large bowl. Stir in the chocolate mixture and vanilla. Add the eggs; mix well. Fold in the walnuts. Pour into an 8-inch-square baking pan sprayed with cooking spray. Bake for 20 to 30 minutes.

Yield: 8 brownies

Blonde Brownies

1 cup flour
½ teaspoon each baking powder and salt
⅛ teaspoon baking soda
⅓ cup butter, melted
1 cup packed brown sugar
1 egg
1 teaspoon vanilla extract
   Nonstick cooking spray
¾ cup butterscotch chips or ¾ cup peanut butter chips plus ¼ cup chopped peanuts

Preheat the oven to 350 degrees. Sift the first four dry ingredients into a bowl. Combine the butter, brown sugar, egg and vanilla in a large bowl. Add the flour mixture. Spread in an 8-inch-square baking pan sprayed with cooking spray. Sprinkle the butterscotch chips or peanut butter chips and peanuts over the top. Bake for 20 to 25 minutes.

Yield: 16 brownies

a memory

This is the first recipe I ever baked and it's been used by my family and friends for over 20 years. I learned how to make this in my high school cooking class. Be sure not to use half a cup of salt instead of half a cup of flour as I did!

Chocolate Pecan Squares

A grown-up version of the classic chocolate chip cookie.

2	cups flour
1	teaspoon baking soda
1/4	teaspoon salt
1	cup shortening
1	cup packed brown sugar
3/4	cup sugar
2	egg yolks
1	tablespoon cold water
1	teaspoon vanilla extract
2	cups chocolate chips
3	egg whites
1	cup chopped pecans

Preheat the oven to 350 degrees. Sift the flour, baking soda and salt into a bowl.

Cream the shortening, brown sugar and 1/2 cup of the sugar in the mixer bowl of an electric mixer at medium speed, scraping the bowl occasionally. Add the egg yolks, water and vanilla, beating until blended. Stir in the flour mixture. Spread evenly in a nonstick 9x13-inch baking pan. Sprinkle the chocolate chips over the batter.

Beat the egg whites in a large mixer bowl at high speed until soft peaks form. Add the remaining 1/4 cup sugar gradually, beating constantly until stiff peaks form. Spread over the chocolate chips.

Sprinkle the pecans over the beaten egg whites. Bake for 25 to 30 minutes or until the edges pull from the sides of the pan. Cool in the pan on a wire rack. Cut into squares.

Yield: 2 dozen squares

Mississippi Mud Bars

Nonstick cooking spray
Flour for dusting
1 cup butter
2 cups sugar
4 eggs
1/3 cup baking cocoa
3/4 teaspoon salt
1 1/2 cups flour

1 teaspoon vanilla extract
1 1/2 cups flaked coconut
1 1/2 cups chopped pecans
9 ounces marshmallow creme
1/2 to 1/3 can dark chocolate fudge frosting

Preheat the oven to 350 degrees. Coat a 9x13-inch baking pan with the cooking spray. Dust with the flour.

Cream the butter and sugar in a large bowl. Add the eggs, one at a time, beating after each addition. Sift the cocoa, salt and flour into a medium bowl. Add to the egg mixture. Stir in the vanilla, coconut and pecans. Pour into the pan.

Bake for 25 to 30 minutes or until a wooden pick inserted in the center comes out clean. Remove from the oven.

Spread the marshmallow creme over the top while still hot. Spoon on the frosting; swirl. Cut into bars.

Yield: 2 dozen bars

Cranberry Pine Nut Biscotti

Wonderful to give as a gift with specialty teas and coffees.

$2^1/4$	cups flour	2	egg whites
1	cup sugar	$1^1/2$	teaspoons vanilla extract
1	teaspoon baking powder	1	(6-ounce) package dried
$1/2$	teaspoon baking soda		cranberries
1	teaspoon cinnamon	$3/4$	cup pine nuts, lightly toasted
$1/2$	teaspoon nutmeg		Flour for shaping
2	eggs		

Preheat the oven to 325 degrees. Combine the first 6 ingredients in a medium mixer bowl. Whisk the eggs, egg whites and vanilla in another bowl. Add to the flour mixture, mixing just until moist, using an electric mixer at medium speed. Mix in the cranberries and pine nuts.

Turn onto a floured surface. Divide the dough in half and pat each half into a log approximately $1^1/2$x14 inches. Place each log on a baking sheet. Bake for 30 minutes or until firm. Cool on a wire rack. Reduce the oven temperature to 300 degrees. Cut the biscotti into $1/2$-inch slices. Stand the biscotti upright on the baking sheet. Bake for 20 minutes. Let cool; store in a loosely covered container.

Yield: $2^1/2$ dozen biscotti

Designer
Ria Zake Jacob

Photographer
Cameron
Carothers

Almond Citrus Biscotti

The taste and texture of these biscotti make them delectable with a cup of tea.

Nonstick cooking spray
$2^3/_4$ cups flour
$1^1/_2$ cups sugar
1 teaspoon baking powder
$^1/_2$ teaspoon salt
1 teaspoon anise seeds

Grated zest of 1 lemon
Grated zest of 2 oranges
3 eggs, beaten
1 teaspoon vanilla extract
Flour for kneading
1 cup slivered almonds, toasted

Preheat the oven to 350 degrees. Coat a baking sheet with the cooking spray. Combine $2^3/_4$ cups flour, sugar, baking powder, salt, anise seeds, lemon zest and orange zest in a large bowl. Mix in the eggs and vanilla. Do not overmix. Turn out onto a floured work surface. Knead in the almonds. Shape into two 2x10-inch logs. Place on the baking sheet. Bake for 40 to 45 minutes. Remove from the oven; let cool. Reduce the oven temperature to 300 degrees. Cut into $^1/_2$-inch slices, and arrange on a baking sheet. Bake for 10 to 15 minutes. Cool. Store in an airtight container.

Yield: $2^1/_2$ dozen biscotti

Forgotten Cookies

2 egg whites, at room
temperature
$^2/_3$ cup sugar
Pinch of salt

1 teaspoon vanilla extract
1 cup chopped pecans
1 cup chocolate chips

Preheat the oven to 350 degrees. Cover a baking sheet with foil.

Beat the egg whites in a large bowl until foamy. Beat in the sugar slowly and gradually, beating until stiff peaks form. Beat in the salt and vanilla. Fold in the pecans and chocolate chips. Drop the dough by teaspoonfuls onto the baking sheet.

Place the baking sheet in the oven. Close the oven door and immediately turn off the heat. Let stand for 12 hours, without opening the oven door.

Yield: 1 to 2 dozen cookies

Coconut Lime Bars

A superb alternative to lemon bars.

1	cup butter or margarine, softened	4	eggs, slightly beaten
1/4	teaspoon salt	1	tablespoon grated lime peel
1/2	cup confectioners' sugar	5	tablespoons fresh lime juice
2 1/4	cups flour	2	cups sugar
		1	cup flaked coconut

Preheat the oven to 350 degrees. Combine the butter, salt, confectioners' sugar and 2 cups of the flour in a bowl, mixing to make a soft dough. Press evenly into an ungreased 9x13-inch baking pan. Bake for 15 to 20 minutes or until golden.

Combine the eggs, lime peel, lime juice, sugar and the remaining 1/4 cup flour in a bowl; blend until smooth. Spoon over the crust. Sprinkle the coconut over the lime mixture. Reduce the oven temperature to 325 degrees. Bake for 25 minutes or until firm. Cool. Cut into bars.

Yield: 3 dozen bars

Pistachio Chocolate Shortbread

	Nonstick cooking spray	3/4	cup semisweet chocolate chips
3/4	cup butter, softened	3/4	cup shelled pistachios, coarsely chopped
1/2	cup sugar		
1	teaspoon vanilla extract	1	egg white, beaten
1 1/2	cups flour		

Preheat the oven to 300 degrees. Coat an 8-inch-square baking pan with the cooking spray.

Cream the butter and sugar in a bowl. Mix in the vanilla. Stir in the flour gradually. Fold in the chocolate chips and 1/2 cup of the pistachios. Spread in the pan. Brush lightly with the egg white. Sprinkle the remaining 1/4 cup pistachios over the batter.

Bake for 30 minutes or until lightly browned. Cool and cut into squares.

Yield: 16 squares

Mocha Oatmeal Bars

Oat Bars

Nonstick cooking spray
1 cup butter or margarine, softened
2 cups packed light brown sugar
3 eggs
1 teaspoon vanilla extract
3 cups quick-cooking oats
2 1/4 cups flour
1 teaspoon baking soda
1/2 teaspoon salt
2 tablespoons baking cocoa

Chocolate Filling

2 cups semisweet chocolate chips
1 (14-ounce) can sweetened condensed milk
2 tablespoons butter or margarine
1/2 teaspoon salt
1 cup chopped walnuts
2 tablespoons espresso powder

For the bars, preheat the oven to 350 degrees. Coat a 10x15-inch jelly roll pan with the cooking spray.

Cream the butter and brown sugar in the large mixer bowl of an electric mixer at medium speed until light and fluffy. Add the eggs and vanilla, beating well. Combine the oats, flour, baking soda and salt in a bowl. Mix into the butter mixture. Spread 2/3 of the mixture in the pan.

For the filling, combine the chocolate chips, condensed milk, butter and salt in a medium saucepan. Cook over low heat until the chocolate chips and butter melt and the mixture is smooth, stirring constantly. Stir in the walnuts and espresso powder. Spread evenly over the oats mixture.

Mix the cocoa into the remaining 1/3 oats mixture. Spoon evenly over the top of the filling. Bake for 20 minutes. Cool. Cut into bars.

Yield: 5 dozen bars

Molasses Cookies

A classic.

3/4	cup shortening		1/2	teaspoon ground cloves
1	cup sugar		1/2	teaspoon ground ginger
1/4	cup molasses		1	teaspoon cinnamon
1	egg		1/2	teaspoon salt
2	teaspoons baking soda			Sugar
2	cups flour			

Cream the shortening and 1 cup sugar in a large bowl. Beat in the molasses. Beat in the egg. Combine the baking soda, flour, cloves, ginger, cinnamon and salt in a bowl. Add to the shortening mixture; mix well. Chill, covered, in the refrigerator for 1 hour.

Preheat the oven to 375 degrees. Shape dough into 1-inch balls and roll in the sugar. Arrange on an ungreased baking sheet. Press each ball twice with fork tines to flatten somewhat and create a crisscross pattern. Bake for 8 to 10 minutes. Let cool completely on a wire rack.

Yield: 4 dozen cookies

Melting Moment Cookies

These cookies will absolutely melt in your mouth.

Cookies

	Nonstick cooking spray
1	cup butter, softened
1/3	cup confectioners' sugar
3/4	cup cornstarch
1	cup flour

Frosting

4	ounces cream cheese, softened
1	cup confectioners' sugar
1	teaspoon vanilla extract
	Food coloring

For the cookies, preheat the oven to 350 degrees. Coat a baking sheet with the cooking spray. Beat the butter in a bowl. Mix in the confectioners' sugar, cornstarch and flour. Shape into small balls and arrange on the baking sheet. Bake for 10 to 12 minutes. Let cool.

For the frosting, cream the cheese, confectioners' sugar and vanilla in a small bowl. Mix in the food coloring. Frost the cookies.

Yield: 2 to 3 dozen cookies

To-Shine-For Sunflower Cookies

A light, crispy cookie.

1	cup packed brown sugar
1	cup shortening
1/4	cup butter, softened
3/4	cup rolled oats
3/4	cup sunflower seed kernels
3/4	cup flaked coconut
1	teaspoon vanilla extract
1	egg
1	cup vegetable oil
1	cup sugar
3/4	cup crisp rice cereal
3	cups flour
1	teaspoon baking soda
1	teaspoon cream of tartar
1/2	teaspoon salt

Preheat the oven to 375 degrees. Combine the brown sugar, shortening, butter, oats, sunflower seed kernels, coconut, vanilla, egg, oil, sugar and cereal in a large bowl.

Combine the flour, baking soda, cream of tartar and salt in a medium bowl. Add to the cereal mixture and mix well.

Shape the dough into small balls and arrange on a cookie sheet. Press each cookie with a fork to flatten slightly. Bake for 9 minutes. Cool for 1 minute before removing from the cookie sheet.

Yield: 4 1/2 dozen cookies

**Designer
Lauren Elia**

**Photographer
Holly
Richmond**

**Pasadena Showcase
House of Design**

White Chocolate Cherry Cookies

1	cup coarsely chopped pecans	1/2	teaspoon salt
9	ounces white chocolate, coarsely chopped	1	cup unsalted butter, softened
1	cup dried tart cherries	2/3	cup sugar
2 1/3	cups flour	2/3	cup packed brown sugar
1	teaspoon baking soda	2	eggs
		1 1/2	teaspoons vanilla extract

Preheat the oven to 350 degrees. Line a cookie sheet with parchment paper.

Combine the pecans, white chocolate and cherries in a bowl.

Sift the flour, baking soda and salt into another bowl.

Cream the butter, sugar and brown sugar in a large bowl until light and fluffy. Add the eggs, one at a time, beating after each addition. Beat in the vanilla. Add the flour mixture, beating just until the mixture is combined. Stir in the pecan mixture.

Shape the dough into 1 1/2-inch balls and arrange them on the cookie sheet, placing them 3 inches apart. Bake on the middle oven rack for 13 to 15 minutes or until golden brown. Remove cookies to a wire rack to cool.

Yield: 4 dozen cookies

Chocolate Chip Cookies with a Secret

The secret to these superb cookies is using cold butter, refrigerating the dough for at least four hours before baking, and keeping the dough cold while baking the cookies in batches.

	Nonstick cooking spray	2¹/2	cups flour
1	cup cold butter	1¹/4	teaspoons baking soda
1	cup packed brown sugar	1	teaspoon salt
³/4	cup sugar	3	cups semisweet chocolate chips
2	large eggs	2	cups chopped walnuts
1¹/2	teaspoons vanilla extract		

Coat a cookie sheet with the cooking spray.

Cream the butter, brown sugar and sugar in a large bowl. Beat in the eggs one at a time. Stir in the vanilla.

Combine the flour, baking soda and salt in a medium bowl. Mix into the creamed mixture. Stir in the chocolate chips and walnuts. Chill, covered, in the refrigerator for 4 to 12 hours.

Preheat the oven to 375 degrees. Drop the dough by 1¹/2-inch balls onto the cookie sheet. Bake for 8 to 10 minutes or until brown.

Yield: 5 to 6 dozen cookies

Almond Cognac Truffles

Use your favorite liqueur to flavor these truffles.

¹/2	pound bittersweet chocolate, chopped	2	large egg yolks
¹/4	cup unsalted butter	1	tablespoon Cognac
		³/4	cup sliced almonds, toasted

Line a baking sheet with waxed paper.

Melt the chocolate in the top of a double boiler over medium heat. Add the butter, stirring until melted. Remove from the heat. Whisk in the egg yolks until glossy. Stir in the Cognac. Chill, covered, until firm. Shape the truffle mixture into small balls; roll the balls in the almonds. Arrange on the baking sheet. Store, covered, in the refrigerator for up to 4 days.

Yield: about 3 dozen truffles

Five Pounds of Easy Fudge

12	ounces German's sweet chocolate, chopped
2	cups semisweet chocolate chips
1	(7-ounce) jar marshmallow creme
$4^1/_2$	cups sugar
1	(12-ounce) can evaporated milk
2	tablespoons butter
$^1/_8$	teaspoon salt
1	tablespoon vanilla extract
2	cups chopped walnuts or pecans

Butter a 9x13-inch dish.

Combine the German's chocolate, chocolate chips and marshmallow creme in the large bowl of an electric mixer.

Combine the sugar, evaporated milk, butter and salt in a heavy 3- or 4-quart saucepan. Bring to a boil over high heat, stirring constantly. When the mixture comes to a boil, lower the heat to medium. Cook for 6 minutes. Keep the mixture boiling steadily and stir constantly. Pour the boiling syrup over the chocolate mixture. Beat at medium speed until the chocolate is melted and the ingredients are well blended. Stir in the vanilla and walnuts.

Pour into the prepared dish. Let cool for 24 hours at room temperature. The fudge will lose its gloss if cooled in the refrigerator. Cut into pieces.

Yield: 5 pounds

Coffee Pecan Toffee

You will never buy toffee again.

1¹/₄ cups unsalted butter
1   cup sugar
¹/₃   cup packed light brown sugar
¹/₃   cup water
1   tablespoon dark unsulfured molasses
2   teaspoons instant espresso powder
¹/₂   teaspoon cinnamon
¹/₄   teaspoon salt
2   cups coarsely chopped pecans, toasted
4¹/₂ ounces bittersweet chocolate, finely chopped
4¹/₂ ounces white chocolate, finely chopped

Butter a small baking sheet. Melt 1¹/₄ cups butter in a heavy
2¹/₂-quart saucepan over low heat. Add the sugar, brown sugar,
water, molasses, espresso powder, cinnamon and salt, stirring
until the sugar and brown sugar dissolve.

Attach a candy thermometer to the saucepan. Increase the heat
to medium. Cook for 20 minutes or until the thermometer
registers 290 degrees, stirring slowly but constantly and scraping
the bottom of the pan with a wooden spatula. Remove from the
heat. Mix in 1¹/₂ cups of the pecans. Pour the mixture
immediately onto the baking sheet; do not scrape the pan. Tilt
the baking sheet so that the toffee spreads to ¹/₄ inch thick.

Sprinkle the bittersweet chocolate and white chocolate by
generous tablespoonfuls over the toffee, alternating the
bittersweet and white chocolate to create a patchwork pattern.
Let stand for 1 minute. Swirl the chocolates with the back of a
spoon to spread slightly. Shake the baking sheet to create an
even chocolate layer. Swirl the chocolates with the tip of a knife
to create a marbled pattern. Sprinkle the remaining ¹/₂ cup
pecans over the chocolates.

Chill, covered, in the refrigerator for 1 hour or until the toffee is
firm. Break into pieces. Serve cold or at room temperature.

Yield: about 2 pounds

a memory

**The first time I made these,
my mom could not stop
snitching them. I felt like I
was the mother telling her,
"Don't spoil your dinner."**

Let's Play

Kids sure know how to have fun—on the playground or in the nursery. Why not have fun in the kitchen, as well? These recipes are kid-friendly, especially quick to prepare, with fewer ingredients and steps involved. Everyone will wear a smile as they are mixing and measuring!

**Designer
Kathleen
Formanack**

**Photographer
Cameron
Carothers**

**Serenity Infant
Care Home**

Corn and Zucchini Quesadilla

May be served as an appetizer or as a light weeknight meal with a fresh salad and bread.

1	tablespoon olive oil	2	tablespoons finely chopped red onion
1	cup fresh or frozen corn		
1/8	teaspoon salt	1	jalapeño, minced (optional)
1/8	teaspoon pepper	1/4	cup julienned zucchini
3	(7-inch) flour tortillas	1/4	cup shredded white or yellow
1/2	cup shredded Monterey Jack cheese		Cheddar cheese

Warm the oil in a large nonstick skillet. Add the corn. Cook for 1 to 2 minutes or just until hot and cooked through, stirring constantly. Season with the salt and pepper.

Preheat the oven to 450 degrees. Arrange 1 tortilla on an ungreased baking sheet. Layer with half the Monterey Jack cheese, onion, jalapeño, corn, zucchini and Cheddar cheese, ending with the Cheddar.

Arrange another tortilla over the top and repeat the layering. Cover with the remaining tortilla. Bake for 4 minutes. Turn the stack over. Bake for 4 to 6 minutes or until the tortillas are slightly crisp and the cheese is melted. Quarter the stack. Serve immediately.

Yield: 4 servings

Beef and Macaroni Delight

Kids love it!

Nonstick cooking spray
1 large onion, chopped
3 ribs celery, chopped
1 pound ground beef
7 ounces elbow macaroni

1 (14-ounce) can stewed tomatoes
1 (10 3/4-ounce) can condensed tomato soup

Preheat the oven to 350 degrees. Coat a nonstick skillet with the cooking spray. Add the onion and celery. Sauté until tender. Add the ground beef. Brown, stirring until the beef is crumbly; drain.

Cook the macaroni according to package directions or until al dente; drain. Add to the beef mixture. Stir in the stewed tomatoes and tomato soup.

Spoon into a baking dish. Bake for 45 minutes or until the mixture bubbles.

Yield: 4 servings

Sweet-and-Sour Meatballs

Meatballs
3 pounds ground beef
1 envelope onion soup mix
2 slices dry or toasted bread, crumbled
Dash of Worcestershire sauce

Sweet-and-Sour Sauce
3 (12-ounce) bottles chili sauce
1 cup grape jelly
1 tablespoon soy sauce
1 teaspoon lemon juice
1/2 teaspoon cornstarch

For the meatballs, preheat the oven to 350 degrees. Combine the ground beef, soup mix, bread crumbs and Worcestershire sauce in a large bowl, mixing well. Shape into 1-inch balls. Arrange on a broiler pan. Broil for 10 minutes.

For the sauce, combine the chili sauce, jelly, soy sauce, lemon juice and cornstarch in an electric slow cooker. Add the meatballs. Cook for 1 to 1 1/2 hours or until heated through.

Yield: 8 dozen meatballs

Children's Table Manners

- *It is a wonderful idea to have a family meal together at least once or twice a week without the television on and without answering the telephone. Bringing the family together promotes punctuality, conversation skills, respect, and cooperation.*

- *Encourage your child to set the table, to remove his napkin once he sits down, to remove his dishes and to push his chair in after a meal.*

- *A child should only begin eating when the parent or host tells him to.*

- *For snack time, always try to give your child a plate and a napkin.*

**Designer
Cynthia
Bennett**

**Photographer
Rachel Olguin**

One-Step Family Lasagna

You don't have to cook the lasagna noodles first—just assemble the dish, cover and bake.

1/2	pound lean ground beef	16	ounces lasagna noodles
3/4	pound hot Italian sausage, casing removed	1	(15-ounce) container part-skim ricotta cheese
1	(26-ounce) jar thick spaghetti or marinara sauce	1	pound mozzarella cheese, shredded
1 1/2	cups water	1	cup grated Parmesan cheese
1/2	cup chopped fresh basil, or 3 scant tablespoons dried		

Preheat the oven to 350 degrees. Sauté the ground beef and sausage in a large heavy skillet over medium-high heat for 4 minutes or until cooked through, stirring until crumbly; drain. Remove to a bowl.

Combine the spaghetti sauce, water and basil in a large bowl. Spread 1 1/2 cups of the sauce mixture in the bottom of a 9x13-inch baking dish. Arrange 1/3 of the noodles, slightly overlapping if necessary, atop the sauce. Layer half the ricotta cheese, mozzarella cheese and meat; top with 1/4 cup of the Parmesan cheese. Spread with 1 1/2 cups sauce. Repeat layering with the noodles, ricotta cheese, mozzarella cheese, meat and 1/4 cup Parmesan cheese. Arrange the remaining 1/3 noodles atop the mixture. Spoon on the remaining sauce. Top with the remaining 1/2 cup Parmesan cheese.

Cover tightly with heavy-duty foil. Place on a baking sheet. Bake for 1 hour or until the noodles are tender and the lasagna is heated through. Uncover; let stand for 15 minutes. Cut into squares and serve.

Hint: May be made 1 day ahead and stored, covered, in the refrigerator. Reheat, covered, at 350 degrees for 45 minutes.

Yield: 8 servings

Chicken Cacciatore with Linguini

4 boneless, skinless chicken breasts, cut into bite-size pieces
Flour
4 tablespoons butter
2 tablespoons olive oil
1 green bell pepper, cut into julienne strips
1/2 medium onion, chopped coarsely
2 cloves garlic, chopped
1 1/2 pounds mushrooms, sliced
2 (14-ounce) cans diced tomatoes in juice
1 cup white wine
1 teaspoon dried oregano
1 teaspoon dried marjoram
1 teaspoon dried thyme
2 teaspoons salt
1/2 teaspoon pepper
2 tablespoons chopped fresh parsley, or 2 teaspoons dried
8 ounces linguini

Preheat the oven to 350 degrees. Coat the chicken with flour. Warm 2 tablespoons of the butter and 1 tablespoon of the oil in a large skillet. Add the chicken. Cook until browned.

Warm the remaining 2 tablespoons butter and 1 tablespoon oil in a large saucepan. Add the green pepper, onion, garlic and mushrooms. Cook for 5 minutes, stirring frequently. Stir in the tomatoes. Stir in the wine, oregano, marjoram, thyme, salt, pepper and parsley.

Arrange the chicken in a 9x13-inch baking dish. Spoon the vegetable mixture over the chicken. Bake, covered, for 45 minutes. Uncover. Bake for 10 minutes.

Cook the linguini according to package directions or until al dente; drain. Serve the chicken over the linguini.

Yield: 4 servings

Oven-Fried Drumsticks

Kids will love these crispy drumsticks; parents will like them, too.

¹/₂	cup soft bread crumbs	1¹/₂	teaspoons dried oregano
¹/₂	cup grated Parmesan cheese	¹/₂	teaspoon salt
3	tablespoons chopped fresh parsley, or 3 teaspoons dried	¹/₄	teaspoon pepper
		¹/₂	cup butter
2	teaspoons onion powder	¹/₄	cup Dijon mustard
1¹/₂	teaspoons paprika	12	chicken drumsticks

Preheat the oven to 350 degrees. Combine the bread crumbs, Parmesan cheese, parsley, onion powder, paprika, oregano, salt and pepper in a large bowl.

Melt the butter in a small saucepan over low heat. Remove from the heat. Whisk in the mustard. Brush the butter mixture over the drumsticks; roll in the bread crumbs, coating all sides.

Arrange the drumsticks on a buttered baking sheet. Bake for 1 hour or until golden brown and cooked through. Serve warm or at room temperature.

Yield: 6 servings

Easy Turkey Potpies

2 cups cooked turkey, cut into 1-inch cubes
1 (8-ounce) package mixed frozen vegetables
1 to 2 cups homemade turkey gravy or canned chicken gravy

Salt and pepper to taste
1 (10-ounce) package puff pastry shells (6 unbaked shells)

Combine the turkey, vegetables and gravy in a saucepan. Season with the salt and pepper. Cook, covered, until hot.

Bake the pastry shells according to package directions; fill with the warmed turkey mixture. Serve with a tossed green salad.

Yield: 6 servings

Dishwasher Salmon

Your kids will enjoy the great taste and the unusual cooking process. They will rush to tell their friends.

1 to 2 pounds salmon
1 tablespoon olive oil
1/2 teaspoon chopped fresh dill

1/2 cup mayonnaise
Juice of 1 lemon

Brush the salmon with the oil. Sprinkle with the dill. Wrap two layers of foil around the salmon. Seal and fold the ends over 3 or 4 times.

Place the salmon in the upper dishwasher rack. Turn to the normal cycle, which should run for about 80 minutes. Cook until a meat thermometer registers at least 160 degrees. Combine the mayonnaise and lemon juice in a small bowl. Serve the salmon hot or at room temperature with the lemon sauce.

Hint: May also use cod, trout or orange roughy steaks instead of salmon.

Yield: 8 servings

Quick Pecan Cake

This is a simple and wonderful after-school snack.

Nonstick cooking spray
1 pound brown sugar
4 eggs

2 cups baking mix
1 teaspoon vanilla extract
1 cup chopped walnuts or pecans

Preheat the oven to 350 degrees. Coat an 8-inch-square baking pan with the cooking spray.

Combine the brown sugar, eggs, baking mix, vanilla and walnuts in a large bowl. Pour into the pan. Bake for 30 minutes.

Yield: 6 servings

Dirt Cake

1/2 cup butter, softened
8 ounces cream cheese, softened
1 cup confectioners' sugar
2 (4-ounce) packages vanilla instant pudding mix

3 1/2 cups milk
1 (12-ounce) container frozen whipped topping
1 (20-ounce) package chocolate sandwich cookies, crushed Gummy worms

Cream the butter, cream cheese and confectioners' sugar in a large bowl.

Combine the pudding mix and milk in another bowl. Stir in the whipped topping. Fold into the cream cheese mixture.

Alternate layers of the cookie crumbs and cream cheese mixture in a serving bowl, ending with the cookie crumbs. Decorate with gummy worms.

Yield: 10 servings

Roll-a-Rolo Cookies

A gooey, rich cookie that the kids will love with a glass of milk. They will also be happy to help unwrap the candies.

Nonstick cooking spray	1 cup packed brown sugar
2¹/₂ cups flour	2 teaspoons vanilla extract
³/₄ cup baking cocoa	2 eggs
1 teaspoon baking soda	¹/₂ cup chopped pecans
1 cup butter, softened	48 Rolo candies, unwrapped
1 cup sugar	

Preheat the oven to 375 degrees. Coat a baking sheet with the cooking spray.

Combine the flour, cocoa and baking soda in a medium bowl.

Cream the butter, sugar and brown sugar in a mixer bowl. Beat in the vanilla, eggs and pecans. Beat in the flour mixture, adding a little at a time.

Wrap 1 tablespoon of the dough around each candy, being certain to completely cover the candy. Arrange on the baking sheet. Bake for 7 to 10 minutes or until browned; the tops may begin to crack slightly. Cool on the baking sheet until firm.

Yield: 4 dozen cookies

Marketing Your Lemonade Stand

If you make your stand fun and inviting, offer a variety of products, and do it with a smile, you should have a very successful day! Here are a few tips:

• *The "Lemonade Stand" sign should be big and preferably handmade by the children. Clearly display what you are selling and what each item costs.*

• *Advertise in advance by distributing fliers to neighbors.*

• *Offer various flavors of lemonade by placing a bit of fruit purée in the cup first and then pouring in the lemonade.*

**Designer
Judy Campbell**

**Photographer
Cameron
Carothers**

Lemon Whipper Snappers

These taste like little cakes.

	Nonstick cooking spray
1	package lemon cake mix, preferably not extra-moist or pudding-style
2	eggs
2	cups whipped topping
1/2	cup confectioners' sugar

Preheat the oven to 350 degrees. Coat a baking sheet with the cooking spray.

Combine the cake mix, eggs and whipped topping in a large bowl.

Shape by tablespoonfuls into balls and roll in the confectioners' sugar. Place on the baking sheet. Bake for 10 to 15 minutes, being careful not to overbrown. Coat the baking sheet with cooking spray before reusing each time.

Yield: 2 to 3 dozen cookies

Monster Cookies

A must for the lunch box.

	Nonstick cooking spray
3	cups peanut butter
1	cup butter, softened
2	cups packed brown sugar
2	cups sugar
6	eggs
1½	teaspoons vanilla extract
9	cups rolled oats
4	teaspoons baking soda
2	cups candy-coated chocolate pieces
1	cup chocolate chips

Preheat the oven to 350 degrees. Coat a baking sheet with the cooking spray.

Cream the peanut butter, butter, brown sugar and sugar in a large bowl. Beat in the eggs and vanilla.

Combine the rolled oats and baking soda. Stir into the butter and sugar mixture; blend thoroughly. Stir in the candy and chocolate chips. Drop by ice cream scoopfuls onto the baking sheet. Bake for 12 to 15 minutes.

Yield: 3 to 4 dozen cookies

No-Bake Fudge Cookies

1½ cups sugar
¼ cup baking cocoa
½ cup milk
1 teaspoon vanilla extract

½ cup butter or margarine
½ cup chopped pecans
3 cups rolled oats
½ cup peanut butter

Combine the sugar, cocoa and milk in a saucepan. Boil for 1 minute; remove from the heat. Stir in the vanilla, butter, pecans, oats and peanut butter.

Drop by teaspoonfuls onto waxed paper. Chill, covered, in the refrigerator.

Yield: 2 dozen cookies

Making Christmas candy to give as gifts for friends and neighbors was a family tradition when I was growing up in western North Dakota. On candy making day, our extended family would get together. Making taffy was our favorite. The taffy is molasses-based, so it starts out brown and has to be pulled until white— or as white as you can get it. As children we were so impatient to start pulling that we would put the pans of taffy out in the snow in our front yard to cool. It was always a competition to see who could get the taffy the whitest. One aunt always won because she pulled with a slow, even rhythm.

Auntie Em's Taffy

2	cups sugar
3	cups packed light brown sugar
1	cup molasses
3	cups light corn syrup
1	cup cream
1	cup water
1/2	cup butter
1/4	teaspoon baking soda
1/2	teaspoon vanilla extract

Butter several jelly roll pans. Attach a candy thermometer to a large saucepan.

Combine the sugar, brown sugar, molasses, corn syrup, cream, water and butter in the saucepan. Cook until the thermometer registers 244 degrees. Remove from the heat. Stir in the baking soda and vanilla. Pour into the jelly roll pans. Let cool enough to handle.

Pull until the taffy is off-white. The taffy becomes whiter the more it is pulled.

Yield: about 5 pounds taffy

Peanut Krackle

A fun recipe for kids to make that adults will also love.

4	cups white chocolate chips	1	cup salted peanuts
2¼	cups crisp rice cereal	1	cup peanut butter
2	cups miniature marshmallows		

Butter a 9x13-inch baking dish.

Spread the chocolate chips in a microwave-safe 4-quart baking dish. Microwave on Medium (about 70 percent) for 3 to 4 minutes or until melted, stirring after each minute. Stir in the cereal, marshmallows, peanuts and peanut butter.

Spread in the baking dish. Let cool and cut into squares.

Yield: about 6 dozen cookies

Ginger Water

½	to ¾ cup packed brown sugar	½	cup cider vinegar
1	teaspoon powdered ginger	1	quart cold water

Dissolve the brown sugar and ginger in the vinegar in a 2-quart jar or pitcher, stirring constantly.

Stir in the water and serve.

Yield: 6 servings

Microwave Caramel Corn

Perfect as a slumber party snack. Let the slumberless kids make this treat during the party.

1	cup packed brown sugar
6	tablespoons butter
1/4	cup white corn syrup
1/2	teaspoon salt
1	teaspoon baking soda
4	quarts popped popcorn

Combine the brown sugar, butter, corn syrup and salt in a microwave-safe 2-quart bowl. Microwave on High until boiling. Cook for 2 minutes. Remove from the microwave; stir in the baking soda.

Place the popped popcorn in a clean large microwave-safe paper bag. Pour the syrup over the popcorn; stir with a large spoon. Close the bag and shake to mix the contents. Microwave, in the bag, on High for 1 1/2 minutes. Shake. Cook for 1 1/2 minutes more. Cool.

Yield: 4 quarts popped corn

Graham Cracker Ice Cream

A great alternative to graham crackers as a snack.

2	pints half-and-half	1	cup sugar
2	cups graham cracker crumbs	2	teaspoons vanilla extract

Combine the half-and-half, crumbs, sugar and vanilla in a large bowl. Pour into a loaf pan.

Freeze, covered, for 2 hours or until crystals begin to form. Stir. Freeze for 10 to 12 hours. Serve with berries or chocolate chips.

Yield: 6 servings

Banana Splits

A yummy treat for kids to make.

4   bananas
Assorted fillings (such as
maraschino cherries, strawberry
jam, chocolate chips, granola)

Small marshmallows
Ice cream or whipped topping

Cut and remove a lengthwise 1-inch-wide strip of skin from each banana. Scoop a small channel in the bananas. Spoon in some fillings and marshmallows. Place on a microwave-safe plate. Microwave for 1 minute. Top with ice cream or whipped topping.

Hint: May instead be baked in a 350-degree oven. Place the filled bananas on foil. Bake for 3 to 5 minutes or until the marshmallows melt.

Yield: 4 servings

Sunshine Play Dough

This play dough is not edible.

2	cups flour
1	cup salt
4	teaspoons cream of tartar
2	cups water
2	tablespoons vegetable oil
2	tablespoons washable liquid tempera paint (fluorescent, if possible), or 10 to 20 drops of food coloring

Combine the flour, salt and cream of tartar in a large saucepan. Stir in the water, oil and paint. Cook over medium heat until elastic and difficult to turn in the pan, scraping the bottom of the pan and turning the dough over and over. Do not overcook, or the dough will be crumbly and dry.

Turn out onto a work surface; cover with a dampened cloth. Let cool for up to 10 minutes; knead. Store in an airtight container.

Yield: 1 batch play dough

School Play Dough

I grew up on this recipe. My mother used it in the sixties while teaching nursery school, and I have used it over and over as a teacher, parent, and volunteer working with children. I share it all the time!

A couple of hints:
- *Do not double the recipe. Make twice, if you need more. Two to three batches will accommodate a classroom or party.*
- *Use kitchen utensils as tools. Rolling pins and cookie cutters will allow for special shapes, and a garlic press makes thin strands perfect for hair, grass, etc.*

Cool Snappy Stretch

Non-edible homemade slimy clay for play.

2   cups white glue
1½ cups water, at room temperature
2   teaspoons 20 Mule Team Borax
1   cup hot water
10   drops of food coloring, or
1½ tablespoons washable liquid tempera paint

Pour the glue into the room-temperature water in a measuring cup, stirring constantly.

Dissolve the borax in the hot water in a separate bowl, stirring constantly. Stir in the food coloring. Pour in the glue mixture, stirring constantly and pouring slowly.

Store in an airtight container.

Elmer's glue will not work for this project.

Yield: 1 batch clay

Tips for Using Cool Snappy Stretch

- *Store airtight in a plastic container in the fridge.*
- *Snappy stretch tends to separate as it sits but regains its elastic texture when again used for play.*
- *The mixture oozes off of a tabletop when left sitting. Use a pan with an edge for play.*
- *Caution: Old clothes are a good idea for this project! If the mixture gets on your clothes, wash out immediately before it dries. Don't go anywhere near carpet.*
- *Supervise small children closely so they don't eat it.*

**Designer
Colleen Boyer**

**Photographer
Cameron
Carothers**

Cookbook Committee 1997-98

Laura Kelso—Chairman
Jane Thompson—Assistant
    Chairman
Nancy Hornberger—Executive
    Liaison
Linda Roth—A Junior League of
    Pasadena President
Hilary Clark—Sustaining Advisor
Carole Klove—Sustaining Advisor
Phyllis Wilburn—Sustaining
    Advisor

Recipe Collection

Sarah Rudchenko—Chairman
Lisa Bolin—Chapter Captain
Heidi Houghton—Chapter Captain
Mary Snider—Chapter Captain
Jill Trojanowski—Chapter Captain
Gwyn Williams—Chapter Captain
    Committee Members
    Wendy Kinney
    Peggy Ireland
    Molly Johnson
    Beatrice Hamlin
    Laurie Patruno
    Elizabeth Downs

Book Production

Alison Alpers—Chairman
Laurie Anne M. Cole—Art Director
Sheree Winslow—Copy Editor
    Committee Members
    Sue Bicknell
    Sue Edmonston
    Elizabeth Edwards
    Nancy Foster
    Cari Hall
    Phyllis Wilburn

Interior Designers

Ann Fletcher ASID
Kathleen Formanack ASID
Diana Clark
    Allied Member ASID

Tasting

Gwyn Williams—Chairman
    Committee Members
    Christina Altmayer
    Christina Arnold
    Tali Arnold
    Teresa Aubert
    Pamela Burt
    Toni L. Callahan
    M. Joanna Crawford
    Heather Creeden
    Sally Creedon
    Lori Newton Cuccia
    Nancy Davis-Maack
    Jacqueline T. Goodman
    Phoenix Gunner
    Ashley Hafer
    Cynthia Hall
    Beth Harker
    Terri Hilliard
    Maria Horner
    Lynne Hunter
    Heidi Johnson
    Sherri Mayhew
    Carolyn McAnally
    Angela McLaren
    Lindsay Monroe
    Ann Murphy
    Gay Norris
    Sara Nowak
    Theresa Overing
    Katherine Petti
    Samantha M. Pietsch
    Cherie Raidy
    Elizabeth Ralston
    Elizabeth Berry Saldebar
    Cathy Tosetti
    Amanda Trocker
    Paula Larimore Vento
    Erin Walsh
    Lorie Washington
    Elizabeth Wiley

Cookbook Committee 1998-99

Ann Murphy—Chairman
Gwyn Williams—Assistant
    Chairman, Business Operations
Julie Echols—Assistant Chariman,
    Marketing/Sales
Edwina Dedlow—Fundraising Director
Amelia Lamb—President, Junior
    League of Pasadena
Susan Barry Baggott—Sustaining
    Advisor
Barbara Ealy—Sustaining Advisor
Phyllis Wilburn—Sustaining Advisor

Business Operations

Alison Alpers
Toni Callahan
Laurie Anne M. Cole
Cynthia Hall
Ramona Howard
Laura Marcin
Kristin Moss
Sara Nowak
KerryAnn Plumer
Salpy Pontrelli
Mary Snider

Marketing/Sales

Michele Ciampa
Lyndsay Cotter
Kimberly Ebner
Stephanie Flagg
Cari Hall
Trish Hannon
Heidi Houghton
Melinda Kinsella
Laurie Levy
Jennifer Odermatt
Caroline Purvis
Carol Rush
Deborah Sekercka
Meshell Sohl
Jane Thompson
Suzy Tobin
Buzzy Waite

Participating ASID Interior Designers

Caroline Baker, Allied Member ASID
745 South Marengo Avenue
Pasadena, California 91106
(626) 796-6670

Cynthia Bennett, ASID
501 Fair Oaks Avenue
South Pasadena, California 91030
(626) 799-9701

Colleen Boyer, ASID
8260 Lorain Road
San Gabriel, California 91775
(626) 286-4111

Ursula Brown, ASID
3769 Berwick Drive
La Canada Flintridge,
    California 91011
(818) 790-2283

Judith Kenyon-Burness, ASID
1755 Warwick Road
San Marino, California 91108
(626) 281-0871

Judy Campbell, ASID
1131 Heatherside Road
Pasadena, California 91105
(626) 796-7853

Diana Clark, Allied Member ASID
677 Burleigh Drive
Pasadena, California 91105
(626) 799-1782

Robin Dorman, Allied Member ASID
4435 Encinas Drive
La Canada, California 91011
(818) 952-0103

Lauren Elia, ASID
1560 East Mountain Street
Pasadena, California 91104
(626) 797-4428

Sammye J. Erickson, FASID
Eric Erickson, ASID
P.O. Box 50528
Pasadena, California 91115
(626) 799-7411
(213) 283-9461

Ann Fletcher, ASID
2734 Carlaris Road
San Marino, California 91108
(626) 799-2089

Kathleen Formanack, ASID
608 West Lemon Avenue
Arcadia, California 97007
(626) 447-9157

John Fremdling, ASID
589 East Green Street
Pasadena, California 91101
(626) 449-0656

Ria Zake Jacob, ASID
815 Old Mill Road
Pasadena, California 91108
(626) 793-9351 Phone/FAX

Traci L. Larsen, ASID
646 Durwood Drive
La Canada, California 91011
(818) 790-8976

Lois Virginia D. Mahar, ASID
1427 Merriman Drive
Glendale, California 91202
(818) 242-0952 Phone/FAX

Michaella S. Scherrer, ASID
873 Cumberland
Glendale, California 91202
(818) 240-2315

Phyllis Tomkins, Allied Member
    ASID
Alice Tompkins, Allied Member
    ASID
905 South First Avenue
Arcadia, California 91006
(626) 574-9000

Edward Turrentine, ASID
70 North Raymond Avenue
Pasadena, California 91103
(626) 795-9964

Maxine White, ASID
4241 Shepherds Lane
La Canada, California 91011
(818) 952-3067

Participating Photographers

Cameron Carothers
1340 Glenwood Road, Suite 8
Glendale, California 91201
(818) 246-1057

Weldon Brewster
Martin Fine
Michael E. Garland
Leland Lee
Mark Lohman
Phillip Nilsson
NTA Associates
Rachel Olguin
Holly Richmond
Lori & Fred Stocker
Alexander Vertikoff

Graphic Artist

Stacey Russakow
Creativend
3715 Market Street, Suite 206
Glendale, California 91208
(818) 248-9853

Contributing Writers

Linda Roth
Pamela Hillings Tegtmeyer
Dr. Fernando Roth

Special Acknowledgments

Gene E. Gregg Jr. ESQ
Port O' Call, Pasadena
John Roberts, Floralculturalist
Loren Brown ESQ
Bill Pellman ESQ
Mary Kenyon, Allied Member ASID
Linda Merrifield Kinninger, ASID
Dina Morgan, Allied Member ASID
Sherry Payne, ASID
Christine Seller, Allied Member ASID
Christine Skinner, ASID
Edna Ulasewicz
Mary Falkingham
Tommy Farmer, Florist
Sheryn Jones, Consultant Cookbook
Resources
Robert and Jacqueline Glasgow
The Beaufort House, Victorian B&B,
North Carolina

The Junior League of Pasadena, Inc. gratefully acknowledges the contributions of all those listed below. The generosity of these friends has made Dining by Design *possible.*

Alison Alpers
Christina Altmayer
Kelli Andrews
Teresa Aubert
Elizabeth Autelli
Connie Avison
Caroline Baker
Barbara Baptie
Shannon Barber-Breckheimer
Judy Barnes
Susan Maile Barrows
Sue Barry
Janice Bea
Beaufort House Bed & Breakfast
Linda Beckner
Sheri Bender
Kathleen L. Bertch
Kim Besen
Sue Bicknell
Anna Deane Bigelow
Jennifer Norton Bigelow
Richard Binder
Annemarie Black
Marcia Blanchette
Mary Blencowe
Lisa Bolin
Joan Salisbury Bolton
Katie Ellen Bolton
Marcia Bonnabel
Cameron Booth
Alice Borhead
Martha Wheeler Bowman
Roz Bowman
Rochelle Brannon
Mardi Breckheimer
Debbie Breedlove
Wendy Broderick
Jamie Brown
Donna Brunjes
Judy Burness
Pamela Burt
Toni L. Callahan
Beth Campbell
Judy Campbell
Katie Carey
Joan L. Carter
Lynn Cassidy

Stephanie Chandler
Susan Chandler
April Lane Chase
Mrs. Bolling Robertson Chinn
Michele Rose Ciampa
Hilary Clark
Patricia Cleek
Laurie Anne M. Cole
Debbi Cordano
Lyndsey Cotter
Mary Emmerling Country
Tricia Crider
Mrs. M. Joanna Crawford
Sally Creedon
Mrs. William L. Creedon
Lori Newton Cuccia
Greg Custer
Katie Darnell
Dolores Dart
Mia Davidson
Suzanne M. Davidson
Mary S. Davis
Mrs. Richard D. Davis
Nancy Davis-Maack
Dahlia DeCamp
Jean Diefenderfer
Elizabeth S. Downs
Clara Driscol
Bob Dulik
Joani Durandette
Christine Price Duvall
Barbara Ealy
Kim Ebner
Sue Edmonston
Elizabeth Edwards
Carrie Engelmann
Patti Faciana
Judy Falkenham
Jane Menendez Fall
Judy Faucett
Ann Finnegan
Lindy Finnegan
Ginnie Fisher
Francis Fitzhugh
Elizabeth Fitzpatrick
Kathleen Anne Flaherty
Robert T. Flaherty

Dorothy Flick
Kathleen Formanack
Berni Fornaciari
Susan M. Foster
Margie Lowe-Francis
Mark Gallaudet
Beth Gerber
Stacy Gewecke
Carolyn Gibbs
Robert and Jacqueline Glasgow
Jacqueline T. Goodman & Family
Jessica Goodman
Goodman Pre-School Day Care
Mia Gottlieb
Allison Gruettner
Phoenix Gunner
Elizabeth Guthrie
Megan Haas
Ashley Hafer
Ruthie J. Hageman
Cari Hall
Cynthia Hall
Jacqui Hallstrom
Beatrice Hamlin
Renee Morgan Hampton
Carlotta Hardey
Beth Harker
Ellen Hatch
Suzy Hazel
Michele M. Hilland
Michelle Ahnstedt Horn
Nancy Hornberger
Sarah Horner
Audrey Houghton
Heidi Houghton
Ramona Howard
Peggy Ireland
Tammy Jacinto
Shirley Jagels
Heidi Johnson
Molly Johnson
Joan Jordan
Linda M. Josephson
Georgie Kajer
Kristin Kaiser
Margaret Kaywell
Peg Hawthorne Kean

Joanne Kelly
Brad Kelso
Grayson Kelso
Katie Kelso
Laura Kelso
Merlin Kelso
Wendy Kinney
Melinda Kinsella
Kate Klimow
Carole Klove
Paula Knop
Joan Knowles
Ruth Kokka
Angela Konrad
Pat Korbel
Amy Krumrey
Amy Lamb
David A. Lamb
Susan Lamp
Mike Levine
Prudence Levine
Sheridan Link
Mildred Lohmann
Therese Louk
Mary Lund
Karen L. Lytell
Amanda Macintosh
Marci Maniker-Leiter
Robyn Ratcliffe Manzini
Cathy Marchio
Kren Marks
Melissa Marona
Sherry Marquardt
Sherri Mayhew
Sandra Mays
Carolyn McAnally
Valerie McAndrews
Jane McAniff
Maura McAniff
Heather McElwee
Angela McLaren
Elaine McNiven
Ms. Pamela Mimms
Lindsay Monroe
Victoria S. Mordecai
Janet Morgan
Kristy Morrell
Kristin Moss
DeEtte Mountford
Ann Murphy

Barbara Murphy
Brett Nausha
Elaine Neve
Carrie Nord
Gay Norris
Sara Nowak
Theresa Overing
Laurie Patruno
Melissa Patterson
Margaret L. Pearson
Christine Pehar
Ann Penn
Kitty Petti
Lori Phillipi
Samantha M. Pietsch
Marie Pinnie
Fran Plotkin
Patricia L. Plunkett
Jill Polsby
Salpy Pontrelli
Judy Post
Susan Presley
Karen Preston
Caroline Henry Purvis
Rosemary Quadrini
Carrie Rabkin
Mrs. Gaynel Rader
Diane Ralston
Elizabeth Ralston
Garth Ramsey
Sharon Ramsey
Terra Rayburn
Sue Reville
Nancy Reynolds
Susie Rhodes
Lynae Rice
Kimberley Roberts
Annelizabeth Q. Rogers
Mrs. Henry Martyn Rollins
Linda Roth
Sarah Rudchenko
Carol Lynne Rush
Michelle Sabourin
Elizabeth Berry Saldebar
LaVone Satzinger
Marian Schmidt
Mrs. John Schoentgen
Barbara Schuler
Deborah Sekers
Christine T. Seller

Nancy Shebel
Kit Shenk
Diane Singer
Pam Small
JoAnn Avison Smith
MaryAnn L. Smith
Maureen Smith
Mary Snider
Trudy Snider
Pamela Stein
Jane Stott
Mary Murray Sullivan
Todd Thiemann
Gladys Thompson
Jane Thompson
Carole Thurston
Phyllis Tomkins
Amanda Trocker
Jill Trojanowski
Edna Ulasewicz
Jan Upton
Jennifer Vanderpool
Annie Van Dyke
Paula Larimore Vento
Judy Waldo
Nancy Walker
Erin Walsh
Teri Ward
Ann Evanilla Wasson
Linda Wehmueller
Lisa Wehmueller
Rose Wehmueller
Ruby Weissman
Jane Wells
Karin L. Wentzel
Debra Whitehouse
Jane Whitmore
Phyllis Wilburn
Elizabeth Wiley
Carol S. Williams
Gwyn Williams
Tracey L. Williams
Joanne Wilson
Sheree Winslow
Emily Wood
Cathy Woolway
Lisa Fragiacomo Yuritich

The editors have attempted to present these family recipes in a format that allows approximate nutritional values to be computed. Persons with dietary or health problems or whose diets require close monitoring should not rely solely on the nutritional information provided. They should consult their physicians or a registered dietitian for specific information.

Abbreviations for Nutritional Profile

Cal — Calories	T Fat — Total Fat	Sod — Sodium
Prot — Protein	Chol — Cholesterol	g — grams
Carbo — Carbohydrates	Fiber — Dietary Fiber	mg — milligrams

Nutritional information for these recipes is computed from information derived from many sources, including materials supplied by the United States Department of Agriculture, computer databanks, and journals in which the information is assumed to be in the public domain. However, many specialty items, new products, and processed foods may not be available from these sources or may vary from the average values used in these profiles. More information on new and/or specific products may be obtained by reading the nutrient labels. Unless otherwise specified, the nutritional profile of these recipes is based on all measurements being level.

- Artificial sweeteners vary in use and strength so should be used "to taste," using the recipe ingredients as a guideline. Sweeteners using aspartame (NutraSweet and Equal) should not be used as a sweetener in recipes involving prolonged heating, which reduces the sweet taste. For further information on the use of these sweeteners, refer to the package.
- Alcoholic ingredients have been analyzed for the basic information. Cooking causes the evaporation of alcohol, which decreases alcoholic and caloric content.
- Buttermilk, sour cream, and yogurt are the types available commercially.
- Cake mixes which are prepared using package directions include 3 eggs and 1/2 cup oil.
- Chicken, cooked for boning and chopping, has been roasted; this method yields the lowest caloric values.
- Cottage cheese is cream-style with 4.2% creaming mixture. Dry curd cottage cheese has no creaming mixture.
- Eggs are all large. To avoid raw eggs that may carry salmonella, as in eggnog or 6-week muffin batter, use an equivalent amount of commercial egg substitute.
- Flour is unsifted all-purpose flour.
- Garnishes, serving suggestions, and other optional information and variations are not included in the profile.
- Margarine and butter are regular, not whipped or presoftened.
- Milk is whole milk, 3.5% butterfat. Low-fat milk is 1% butterfat. Evaporated milk is whole milk with 60% of the water removed.
- Oil is any type of vegetable cooking oil. Shortening is hydrogenated vegetable shortening.
- Salt and other ingredients to taste as noted in the ingredients have not been included in the nutritional profile.
- If a choice of ingredients has been given, the profile reflects the first option. If a choice of amounts has been given, the profile reflects the greater amount.

Pg. No.	Recipe Title (Approx Per Serving)	Cal	Prot (g)	Carbo (g)	T Fat (g)	% Cal from Fat	Chol (mg)	Fiber (g)	Sod (mg)
16	Apricots with Gorgonzola	37	1	2	3	60	4	<1	80
17	Eggplant Spread on Parmesan Toasts	49	1	3	4	68	1	1	59
19	Garlic Prawns	274	30	2	15	52	276	<1	384
20	Crab Salad in Endive	87	5	6	5	50	21	4	101
26	Tangy Tofu Dip (per tablespoon)	26	1	1	2	70	0	<1	104
33	Red Pepper Pesto with Crostini	136	2	6	12	78	0	1	68
49	Cranberry Orange Scones	150	3	28	3	18	<1	1	228
51	Cranberry Bran Muffins	361	6	62	11	26	37	3	389
53	Bed and Breakfast Granola	621	10	92	26	37	0	9	38
63	Autumn Pumpkin Pancakes	126	4	14	6	44	30	1	222
71	Light and Lively Gazpacho	105	3	14	5	40	0	3	542
77	Italian Roasted Pepper Soup	280	20	33	6	21	23	2	1670
81	Vegetable Chili	218	7	37	7	26	0	8	412
88	Apple and Bleu Cheese Tossed Salad	388	8	25	30	68	13	4	589
90	Tangy Spinach Salad	567	10	38	44	67	113	5	423
91	Red Potato and Onion Salad	272	6	32	16	49	17	4	126
92	Quick and Easy Salad with Spring Greens and Gorgonzola	272	6	13	23	74	13	2	436
97	Turkey Salad with a Twist	381	29	41	13	29	42	5	2060
99	Black Bean and Corn Fiesta Salad	195	5	21	12	51	0	5	435
103	Couscous Salad	326	6	29	21	57	12	3	197
105	Summer Salad	682	29	62	36	47	58	4	238
115	Roasted Pepper Pasta Sauce	243	6	24	15	53	1	4	1307
119	Herbed Ricotta and Rotelle	574	31	76	16	25	43	3	396
127	Asian Shrimp and Angel Hair Pasta	356	24	42	9	23	135	1	581
128	Spicy Seafood and Shells	530	25	79	13	21	103	5	567
129	Sun-Dried Tomatoes and Feta over Spaghetti	558	48	65	11	19	171	3	1054
132	L.A.-Style Black Beans	316	10	31	18	49	0	10	933
133	Fourth of July Baked Beans	506	14	62	25	43	40	9	1341
133	Green Beans and Peppers with Almonds	90	3	11	5	45	0	4	6
137	Grilled Vegetables with Five-Alarm Marinade*	268	2	17	18	65	0	1	996
138	Peas with Pancetta	149	7	15	7	43	4	5	239
141	Peppers with Almonds	184	2	18	12	57	0	3	5
147	Barley Casserole	302	9	29	18	51	31	6	579
148	Basil Couscous with Summer Squash	125	4	19	4	26	0	3	440
150	Risotto with Portobello Mushrooms	592	16	73	23	35	22	4	1338
153	Lemon Rice	221	7	38	4	17	8	1	488
159	Roast Pork with Apple Topping	412	52	20	12	28	133	1	592
161	Chili-Spiced Pork Tenderloin	414	52	19	14	30	133	<1	603
176	Herb Baked Lamb Chops	496	41	8	31	59	159	1	472
177	Hot Lamb Satay with Mint and Garlic	348	23	32	13	34	76	1	698
179	Roasted Chicken with Fresh Herbs	254	36	1	11	39	108	<1	399
180	Tangy Orange Chicken	406	56	29	6	15	146	1	794
184	Fourth of July Barbecue Chicken	271	34	13	8	27	101	<1	429
185	Grilled Balsamic Chicken	299	38	11	11	33	108	<1	383
187	Bourbon-Laced Chicken with Peaches	288	29	18	10	28	89	3	420
202	Turkey Spinach Meat Loaf	226	21	12	10	41	161	2	477
203	Grilled Halibut	760	30	4	70	82	94	<1	507
207	Spanish Paella	489	26	64	12	23	59	2	608
208	Caribbean Swordfish with Thai Banana Salsa	339	26	32	12	31	45	2	1277
211	Spicy Cajun Shrimp	103	8	4	6	53	64	1	450
216	Golden Apple Crisp	293	2	55	8	24	21	2	183
216	Apricot Poached Pears	220	1	48	2	7	0	5	3

*Nutritional profile includes entire amount of marinade but does not include vegetables.

*See nutritional profile on page 299.

*See nutritional profile on page 299.

*See nutritional profile on page 299.

*See nutritional profile on page 299.

For order information call 1-626-796-0162.

*See nutritional profile on page 299.